UPON THIS ROCK

THE KINGDOM OF GOD,
THE VOICE OF GOD,
AND
THE THIRD REFORMATION

DR. TIM HAMON

Christian International Publishing
Santa Rosa Beach, Florida

First Printing: 2017

ISBN: 978-0-939868-31-5

Cover design by Amani Hanson (Becoming Studios).

Editing, text design and typesetting by Jim Bryson (JamesLBryson@gmail.com).

Proofreading by Lydia Lovett.

Christian International Publishing
P.O. Box 9000
Santa Rosa Beach, Florida 32459
800-388-5308
www.christianinternational.com

Endorsements

Upon this Rock is a much-needed book for every believer! Many people are talking about reforming nations but few have laid down the biblical grid to understand our role in this kingdom work. I encourage anyone interested in the biblical call to make disciples of nations and see God's will done in the earth to read this book!

Dr. Cindy Jacobs
Generals International

A powerful and unstoppable invasion has begun on the earth! It is being propelled by the game-changing revelation that Christians should stop going to church and instead, be the church everywhere they go. Tim Hamon does a brilliant job of enlightening us on how kingdom-minded believers can leaven their world with the unstoppable principles of the kingdom of heaven. You are called to do more than make a difference; you are called to be the difference. This book will teach you how.

Dutch Sheets, Best-selling author
Dutch Sheets Ministries

In *Upon This Rock,* Dr. Tim Hamon opens the Scriptures in a fresh new way to explain Jesus' famous response to Peter: *"Upon this rock I will build my church."* I congratulate Tim for having the courage to tackle this oft-discussed passage and for bringing to light a fresh and potentially unifying understanding of the centuries-old debate. (I won't reveal what Tim says. You'll have to read the book to find out.) I wholeheartedly support Tim in his pursuit of this knowledge and its ramifications regarding the Kingdom of God and the world we live in. The final revival is coming. Dr. Tim Hamon is helping to usher it in.

Dr. Harold R. Eberle
Worldcast Ministries

Tim Hamon has a background in engineering. He thinks linearly, directly, and measures words very carefully. His recent book, *Upon This Rock: The Kingdom of God, The Voice of God, and The Third Reformation*, reflects those characteristics. It is clearly presented, clearly defined, and uses words that cannot be misinterpreted. His connection between the theology of the Kingdom and both the spiritual content of humanity and the management of man's social systems, which comprises the general borders of God's Kingdom on earth is so clear in his presentation that the inevitability of a Third Reformation becomes obvious. In truth, that Reformation has already started and it is growing globally as true leaders in the church continue to wrestle with what it means to "disciple nations." I am grateful to Tim, as this book will undoubtedly stimulate the process and move that Reformation along.

Dr. Dennis Peacocke
Founder, GoStrategic & The Statesmen Project

In this excellent book, by my friend and colleague Dr. Tim Hamon, life in the Kingdom of God is presented with fresh insight. *Upon This Rock* contributes to the dialog of what the church is about—the importance of hearing God's voice, and influencing the world in which we live for the glory of God.

I have often meditated on Jesus' conversation with Nicodemus in John 3. Of special interest is Jesus' statement that one must be born again, or born from above (heaven) in order to see the Kingdom. Nicodemus heard Jesus' voice, understood the words, but struggled with the meaning. As a leader of the Jews, he longed for the Kingdom, (mainly a renewal of David's Kingdom), and certainly believed he would know it if he saw it, but having eyes to see, he did not. Only spiritual eyes, opened though hearing and embracing the Word, would allow him to see it, let alone enter and function in it. Seeing is one thing, entering is another. Both require the Spirit, but what will we see and how are we to function once in the Kingdom of God?

As we move forward in the Third Reformation, we need clear guidance and wisdom from above. This timely work moves us in that direction.

Stan E. DeKoven, Ph.D., MFT
President, Vision International University
Author, *That's the Kingdom of God*

Dr. Tim Hamon is considered one of the best theologically-sound teachers of our day; he accurately teaches biblical doctrine and shares revelation based on the truth of Scripture sans an undertone of denominational, eschatological, historical or cultural bias. He concisely and systematically explains the restoration of the Church within the framework of Historical Context, Revelation, Activation, Technology and Economics. The aggregation of these concepts helps the reader gain a better understanding of God's mandate to *"hear Him"* and how obedience to *"hear Him"* is the catalyst for individual and Church reformation, i.e., the catalyst for cultural reformation and the transformation of nations. As Dr. Hamon states, "All communication that is from God must align with the principles and character of God as described in Scripture. No exceptions".

Remarkably, in the midst of what feels like a concise study of biblical and church history – Paradise Lost to Paradise Regained – Dr. Hamon delivers a beautiful story; a narrative of God's plan for restoration, reformation, and transformation, ultimately culminating in the manifestation of the sons of God (Romans 8:19). It is not formulaic; it is a compelling, encouraging and liberating message; moreover, it is a clarion call for followers of Christ to respond to God's voice and directives: unite and co-labor as one body, be an awakening light within the darkness of embattled cultural wars, engage in the transformation of nations.

I would recommend this book to anyone who is interested in or considers themselves an expert in kingdom theology, church history, or social and cultural transformation.

Kimberly C. Thomas
CEO, Global Advisors Development Group

Books have been written on the Seven Mountains, kingdom, and societal transformation but none with the clarity and insight of *Upon This Rock*. With every page comes greater understanding of what God has done and is now doing on planet earth. Dr. Tim Hamon has laid out sound biblical principles explaining the kingdom of God manifested on the earth, how we hear God to expand the kingdom and what God wants us to be doing now to transform our culture in preparation for His return. *Upon This Rock* reveals the reformation, in which we are now living, as the culmination of all previous reformations and challenges for the church to switch from a role of passively waiting for Christ's return to aggressively working to expand the kingdom of God on the earth until "The kingdoms of this world have become the kingdoms of our Lord and of His Christ, and He shall reign forever and ever!"

Dave Carey
Founding Pastor, Word of Life Christian Center
Apostolic Overseer of Advancing Ministerial Empowerment Network

Dr. Tim writes with an excellent view of today's church; both where it is and where it needs to go. His intellect and humor are well mixed to both teach you and make you smile along the way. There are other books about the Kingdom of God and the Seven Mountain Movement, but not like this one. It is both historically and biblically thorough, and practical enough to actually have action steps for the future. Get a cup of coffee and an Almond Joy bar (Chapter 8) and enjoy.

Rich Marshall
Author: *God@Work and God@Work II*

Dr Tim Hamon has a brilliant mind with the ability to grasp the theological and societal complexities necessary for true societal change. Several years ago I preached on the Kingdom at Vision Church, Destin, Florida. After the message, Tim's father, Bishop Bill Hamon, declared in the Spirit that the Third Reformation was birthed that evening in that convention (The International Gathering of Apostles and Prophets or IGAP).

Hence, Dr Tim is well aware of the implications of the Third Reformation as he was part of that historic moment. As a Pentecostal scholar, Tim has a vast understanding of both experiential and theological nuance which makes this book a practical manifesto that every serious believer should read!

Dr Joseph Mattera
Director, United States Coalition of Apostolic Leaders

For more than 25 years, I have had conversations with Dr. Tim concerning the Saints movement, Kingdom of God, and the Seven mountains of culture.

This message has been his passion. So I expected this book to be good. But by the time I finished reading the first chapter, the fresh way he linked scriptures with the Kingdom of God had already expanded and aligned me in a new way.

I love theory, but I love practical application more. This book brings practical application that the Body of Christ has been missing. For all readers this book will influence your sphere and world. But for church leaders this will deepen and develop your message to mobilize others. I have already taught the first chapter and I am looking forward to Dr. Tim's next book.

Dr. Sharon Stone
Pioneering Overseer, Christian International Europe

In his book, *Upon This Rock*, Dr. Tim Hamon releases keen insight into how the voice of God brings Kingdom impact into culture and society. I have always loved his insightful teaching, combined with a thorough understanding of scripture and history, which will empower the reader to embrace third reformation concepts and thereby change your world. Dr. Tim Hamon is an excellent prophetic teacher. His ability to make scripture come alive with modern cultural relevance brings an equipping perspective to God's call to the church as His change agents in the kingdoms of this world. Upon This Rock is a powerful and practical transformation tool that every believer who loves the Kingdom of God must read.

Jane and Tom Hamon
Vision Church @Christian International

As a teacher I was delighted with the jewels of revelatory truth found throughout this book.

As a pastor I appreciate Tim Hamon and Christian International's commitment to unveil truth that supports and builds the local church.

As a prophet I hear the clear sound of a trumpet from Heaven declaring a Third Reformation and a conviction to "hear and see" what my role is to bring awakening, transformation, and to build His Church "Upon This Rock." Thank you Dr. Tim for this important work.

Patrick Sparrow
ACTs Churches International

Appreciation

THANK YOU ALL!

Thank you, dear reader, for reading this book and special thanks for reading this "Thank you" section. I didn't know if anyone would. I know I hardly ever do. The following is my thanks to all (I hope) the people who helped me get this done. I'll try to take this in more or less chronological order. Thank you.

Thanks, obviously, to God for everything. The Holy Spirit gets credit for all the revelation in this book. Any errors are mine or my editor's. Thank you to my mom and dad: Bishop Bill and Evelyn Hamon. My father has been an inspiration and my mom a constant encouragement. Many thanks to Karen, my wife of 37 years, for constant support and patience while I wiled away the hours trying to write. To my children (Ruth & Jason, Sheri & Rich, Sarah, and Tim II) and grandchildren (Cyrus, Grace, Ian, Ezra, Eli): you deserve thanks, as do my siblings (Tom & Jane Hamon, Sherilyn Hamon-Miller), my friends (can't name them all but will mention Stan DeKoven, Kimberly Thomas, Pat Sparrow) and all my staff at Christian International—Thank you.

Finally, thank you to my editor, Jim Bryson, who helped me finally finish a long drawn-out project.

Thank you,

Dr Tim Hamon

Contents

Prologue

Welcome to my journey of discovery.

I was born in church. Well, I was born in a hospital but my parents lived in a church. Close enough? I grew up the son of a preacher man, blessed to be intensely grounded in the Word of God and his Holy Spirit. As a child, I stood beside Dad and quoted scripture on cue while he preached. In my teenage years, I was often with Dad as he ministered prophetically to hundreds of people. Given my background, it would have been easy and natural for me to go the expected route of Bible school and following my father in to ministry, but God had other plans.

You see, I have an analytical mind and enjoy math and science. Yes, I am a geek. So when college time came, the Lord provided a scholarship to a renown school for a three-year bachelor's program in engineering. Upon graduation, I spent the next 10 years as an engineer working on mainframe computers. Just as the digital age was taking off, however, the Lord intervened and called me into full-time ministry with my family.

I tell you this to explain my approach to revelation. My Christian roots are in classic evangelical theology with a Pentecostal experience. My education and work experience, however, is empirical, applying the scientific method supported by math and logic. So when God wants to reveal something to me, He uses the brain I was born with and the spirit I was born-again with. Typically, He gives me questions to answer like math problems or puzzles to solve. He then leads me step by step through the scriptures until the answer is obvious…even to a geek.

This is my journey. In truth, we are all on a journey, some for hours and some for years. Each journey builds on the discoveries of the past, leading to an exploration of the nature of God and His intentions for the world and His people.

In *Upon This Rock*, I will be sharing some of my most significant discoveries. May you enjoy our journey and the treasures found.

Foreword

By Dr. Bill Hamon

Dr. Tim Hamon, my son, is an Apostolic Teacher of deep comprehension who writes as he teaches. His prose flows with simple logic, profound insight, and a feather touch that belies the weight of its impact. As a master craftsman, Dr. Tim lays a secure foundation, examining all aspects of his subject matter before culminating in truth that is both simple to comprehend and a wonder to behold. It's not uncommon to hear people exclaim, "Wow, I never saw that before!" (No wonder he sells out his CD's and DVD's at our conferences long before any other speaker.)

This is why his latest book is a must-read for all aspiring Third Reformation Kingdom Reformers. Those whom God calls, He also equips. Dr. Tim's work is a crucial component of that equipping. It is the book many have been seeking to understand the practical realities of the Kingdom of God.

Fundamental to his insights, Dr. Tim explains how the kingdoms of this world will become the kingdoms of the Lord, as foretold in Revelation 11:15. In my book on the third and final church reformation, I emphasized the Kingdom of God but I didn't explain what the Kingdom of God is or how we can fulfill the Lord's prayer of "Thy Kingdom come, Thy will be done on Earth as it is in heaven." Instead, I said it would take another book to explain the Kingdom of God and how we achieve it. *Upon This Rock*, by Dr. Tim, is that other book.

Dr. Tim Hamon presents truth that will bring enlightenment, revelation, and new biblical understanding to your life and ministry. Bless you, Tim, for making known to the Body of Christ what God has revealed to you.

What the father has revealed, the son has fulfilled.

Bishop Bill Hamon

Dr. Bill Hamon is the founder and bishop of Christian International Apostolic Network. He has authored 13 major books focused on restoration movements that have taken place during the last 40 years, including: the Prophetic Movement, the Apostolic Movement, the Saints Movement, and the 3rd Reformation. His latest book in 2016 is God's World War III.

Introduction

The Kingdom of God on earth was central to Jesus' life and ministry. He preached the Kingdom message long before He introduced the church (ecclesia). It was a message that resonated with the Jewish culture oppressed by Rome and hungry for the restoration of the kingdom of Israel. For hundreds of years following Jesus' resurrection, and with the understanding that his kingdom was spiritual in nature, ardent believers carried the kingdom message to the surrounding Greco/Roman culture. The influence of those pioneers can be felt even now.

However, the church receded from culture, especially in the 20th century.

Today, in preparation for the return of Jesus Christ, God has restored the revelation of the kingdom message, revealing that the Kingdom of God must manifest in our culture and society, not just in our lives or churches.

Christ's first coming was a *time of reformation* to form a greater and *more perfect tabernacle* (Hebrews 9:10-11). Now we are seeing how great that tabernacle is to be. The church is called to engage our culture and effect its transformation. Jesus is raising up a church that will continue to reform culture until the kingdoms of this world become the kingdoms of our God.

> *Then the seventh angel sounded: And there were loud voices in heaven, saying, "The kingdoms of this world have become the kingdoms of our Lord and of His Christ, and He shall reign forever and ever!"*

Revelation 11:15

The message of the kingdom of God resonates in the earth today, reaching the seven mountains of our culture with a clarion call that will not cease until it has accomplished all God has decreed.

Upon This Rock: The Kingdom of God, The Voice of God, and The Third Reformation is my response to that call. Let's take our mountains. Let's transform our world and establish God's kingdom on earth.

Welcome to the journey.

1

Culture Wars

We are at war.

Just as every war has at least two sides, so there is an opposing force to the establishment of the Kingdom of God. That side promotes a culture that does not recognize God or His purposes.

We see this conflict every day in political debates, protests, appeals to common sense and reason, and promises of enlightenment and harmony. Under the banners of *freedom of religion, freedom from religion, my body—my choice,* or *marriage by convenience,* false values are promulgated throughout all areas of life. The opposing army marches largely unhindered into the cultures of our world, promoting a religion of no-religion and a god of non-existence.

We are in a culture war.

The Kingdom message engages this conflict, seeking the transformation of our culture to conform to the King's authority—God's authority—making the world's kingdoms the kingdoms of our Lord. However, before we can fully engage, we must define "culture" and understand why it is worth fighting for.

"Culture" is briefly defined as follows:

> ...the pattern of human knowledge, belief, and behavior that depends on the capacity for learning and transmitting knowledge to succeeding generations; the customary beliefs, social forms, and material traits of racial, religious, or social group; the characteristic features of everyday existence (way of life) shared by a people in a place or time; the set of attitudes, values, goals, and practices that characterizes an institution or organization.

(Merriam-Webster, 2013)

A more concise picture of world culture comes from the metaphor of the Seven Mountains of Culture. Conceived by Bill Bright and Loren Cunningham in 1975, each of the Seven Mountains represents a major cultural influence. They are:

- Religion
- Government
- Business
- Family
- Media
- Arts/entertainment
- Education.

The Seven Mountains describe the significant influence centers within our culture. From scripture, we understand that these seven strategic areas comprise all of society and must be possessed to establish the Kingdom of God before the return of Jesus Christ. Indeed, the call to action from Joshua 14:12 is:

Now therefore, give me this mountain of which the Lord spoke in that day; for you heard in that day how the Anakim were there, and that the cities were great and fortified. It may be that the Lord will be with me, and I shall be able to drive them out as the Lord said.

As we prepare to answer this call, our fundamental questions must be:

- What is the biblical basis for this war?
- How are we to apply the Seven Mountains to the Kingdom Message?
- What exactly *is* the Kingdom Message?

Let's delve into scripture and discover what God is calling us to accomplish.

2

The Mountain of the Lord's House

Mountains are impressive, are they not? We gaze at them from a distance. We stand in awe at their majesty. We climb them because…well, because they are there! God obviously likes mountains; He made enough of them. But is there more to mountains than just physical beauty and adventure? What is God telling us through mountains?

Mountains in scripture have significant meaning, literally and figuratively. They often represent power or influence, for both God and the ungodly.

> *Those who trust in the Lord are like Mount Zion, which cannot be moved, but abides forever.*
>
> Psalms 125:1

> *Blow the trumpet in Zion, and sound an alarm in My holy mountain!*
>
> Joel 2:1

> *For as you drank on My holy mountain, so shall all the nations drink continually;*
>
> Obadiah 1: 16-21

Then I looked, and behold, a Lamb standing on Mount Zion, and with Him one hundred and forty-four thousand, having His Father's name written on their foreheads.

Revelation 14:1

There are over 450 biblical verses referring to mountains. Nearly every book of the Old Testament has at least one mountain verse, as do nine books of the New Testament. Of course, many of these references point to the *physical* qualities of mountains:

- Noah's Ark came to rest on Mount Ararat, the first of the dry land to appear after the flood. (Better than a valley.)

- The 10 Commandments were given on Mount Sinai, offering privacy for Moses and God to commune.

- Jesus prayed on the Mount of Olives, a place of solitude.

- Jerusalem was built on Mount Zion, a sturdy geological foundation as well as an unassailable fortress. (At least until the Romans got there.)

Yet fewer than half of Old Testament mountain scriptures are found in the narrative books (Genesis through Nehemiah). Most are in the wisdom books (Psalms, Proverbs, Ecclesiastes, Song of Solomon, and Job) and the books of the major prophets (Isaiah, Jeremiah, Ezekiel, and Daniel) and minor prophets (Hosea, Joel, Amos, Obadiah, Jonah, Micah, Nahum, Habakkuk, Zephaniah, Haggai, Zechariah, and Malachi). Further, these mountains are not mentioned for their physical properties but for their greater spiritual meaning.

They shall not hurt nor destroy in all My holy

mountain, for the earth shall be full of the knowledge of the Lord as the waters cover the sea.

Isaiah 11:9

"You were the anointed cherub who covers; I established you; You were on the holy mountain of God; you walked back and forth in the midst of fiery stones.

Ezekiel 28:14

The Lord's Mountain

As incredible as these mountain scriptures are, the one that speaks directly to me concerning the Seven Mountains of Culture is in Isaiah 2 (also repeated Micah 4).

Now it shall come to pass in the latter days that the mountain of the LORD'S house shall be established on the top of the mountains, and shall be exalted above the hills; and all nations shall flow to it. Many people shall come and say, "Come, and let us go up to the mountain of the LORD, to the house of the God of Jacob; He will teach us His ways, and we shall walk in His paths." For out of Zion shall go forth the law, and the word of the LORD from Jerusalem.

Isaiah 2:2-3

Isaiah clearly uses the mountain as a picture of influence in the lives of people. Not just individuals but people groups or nations. Let's look at this verse in detail and understand where God is leading us as we turn our attention to the seven mountains of culture.

"the mountain of the Lord's house..."

Obviously a spiritual mountain, not physical.

"shall be established on top of the mountains..."

A mountain atop other mountains—a picture of influence or dominion.

"in the latter days..."

We could interpret this as God's influence (mountain) dominating over other influences (mountains) in the last days.

"nations shall flow to it [the Lord's house]..."

"Nation" is translated from the Hebrew *gôy*. It refers to a people group with a cultural identity, not necessarily a geopolitical identity. As a unique culture, they have origin, language, norms and governance. The Hebrew people of the Old Testament were a great example of *gôy*. Clearly, they possessed a steadfast cultural identity even as their geopolitical identity waxed and waned.

Unlike the Hebrew *gôy*, the Greek *ethnos* can mean a nation such as Mexico or a people group such as the Mayans. So "nations" could refer to a people group of one of the Seven Mountains: education, religion, family, media, arts/entertainment, government, or business. Let's look at it again with that mindset:

> Many people shall come and say, "Come, and let us
> go up to the mountain of the LORD, to the house of
> the God of Jacob. He will teach us His ways, and we
> shall walk in His paths." For out of Zion shall go forth
> the law, and the word of the LORD from Jerusalem.
>
> Isaiah 2:3

What is happening in this stirring description? First, people are being drawn *from* the other mountains *to* God's mountain. But why? Because it's there? No. They are coming to God's house specifically to be taught His ways and to walk in His paths—to hear and obey. *"For out of Zion shall go forth the law, and the word of the LORD from Jerusalem"* (Isaiah 2:3).

Now we see how the people will be trained.

- teach us Gods ways

- walk in His paths

- the law and the word of the LORD

A brief study reveals some interesting word choices here. The Hebrew word for "law" is *torah,* a precept or statute (Strong's); direction, teaching, and instruction (Vine's). It is like the Greek word *logos,* meaning: the written word of God… what God *has said.*

The Hebrew for "word" is *dabar;* a word by implication spoken (Strong's). *Dabar* means to speak or say (Vine's). *Dabar* is like the Greek *rhema:* the spoken word of God… what God *is saying.*

Hence, the people coming to the mountain of mountains need both: the teaching of scripture which is *logos/torah* to know God's ways, and the hearing of the voice of God, *rhema/dabar* to walk God's paths.

So what's our takeaway from this? The mountain of the Lord's house shall be above all other mountains of culture. Further, its influence shall be greater. And for what purpose? For the nations to hear the Word of God, learn His ways, and walk in His paths.

We are beginning to see the task set before us.

Mountains, Nations, Kingdoms

Matthew 4 describes another mountain—the place of Jesus' temptation. He has just been baptized by John and is immediately led by the Spirit into the wilderness to fast 40 days. (Not the best inducement for a baptismal service, but this is Jesus.) At the end of the fast, Satan comes with three temptations.

> *Again, the devil took Him up on an exceedingly high mountain, and showed Him all the kingdoms of the world and their glory. And he said to Him, "All these things I will give You if You will fall down and worship me." Then Jesus said to him, "Away with you, Satan! For it is written, 'You shall worship the Lord your God, and Him only you shall serve"*
>
> Matthew 4:8-10, NKJV

Let's break down the temptations.

- Turn stones to bread—Jesus' personal needs.

- Protection from harm—Jesus' relationship with the Father.

- The kingdoms of the world—Jesus' position on Earth.

First, notice where Satan takes Jesus: up on a mountain. From here, they can see all the kingdoms of the world. Of course, this is no literal mountain; it's a spiritual place much like the mountain described in Isaiah 2 where all the nations/kingdoms learn of God.

It is from this vantage point that the devil offers the world's kingdoms to Jesus. Interestingly, Jesus does not dispute Satan's power to make the offer. Instead, Jesus rejects the condition that He worship Satan. He further dismisses His tempter as if no other temptation could succeed now that this temptation has failed. One senses that it wasn't about the kingdoms at all.

Frankly, the third temptation always puzzled me. The first two seem more obvious—challenging Jesus' power to make provision and then challenging His relationship with the Father. The third temptation regards prosperity—Jesus' ownership and authority over the earth and its kingdoms. It seems like a weak offer on Satan's part to tempt Jesus with something Jesus already knows is His inheritance.

Then I finally realized that the real temptation is in the way Jesus takes authority. Satan is offering a shortcut to Jesus. *Worship me and I'll give you your inheritance without the cross.* We know this is tempting for Jesus since He confronts it again at Gethsemane. *"He went a little farther and fell on His face, and prayed, saying, 'O My Father, if it is possible, let this cup pass from Me; nevertheless, not as I will, but as You will'"* (Matthew 26:39). While the first two temptations are about Jesus as God's Son, the final temptation is about Jesus as our King.

Once Jesus successfully meets Satan's challenge, He returns to Galilee on fire with His message. *"From that time Jesus began to preach and to say, 'Repent, for the kingdom of heaven is at hand'"* (Matthew 4:17). Jesus passed the kingdom test and began His ministry preaching the kingdom message. You could say He staked His claim on the mountain of God.

Seven Mountains—Good or Evil

The image of God's mountain resting atop the Seven Mountains of culture is compelling, especially since the enemy seeks to usurp God's position from there. In Revelation 17, the seventh angel describes a *"great harlot"* sitting on seven mountains and many waters.

"Come, I will show you the judgment of the great harlot who sits on many waters (v1).

And I saw a woman sitting on a scarlet beast which was full of names of blasphemy, having seven heads and ten horns. (v3).

Verse 9 explains the image:

"Here is the mind which has wisdom: The seven heads are seven mountains on which the woman sits."

Verse 15 continues:

"The waters which you saw, where the harlot sits, are peoples, multitudes, nations, and tongues."

Notice the similarity between Revelation 17 and Isaiah 2, the exception being the great harlot in Revelation is trying to replace the Lord's house to influence the people. Historically, the great harlot represents Rome—the city built on seven hills. *"And the woman whom you saw is that great city which reigns over the kings of the earth"* (Revelation 17: 18). In this scripture, Rome represents the seat of secular culture and influence in the nations.

Just as God seeks to control the kingdoms of the earth, so the enemy wants to control the earth through the mountains of influence. And just as Jesus withstood him, so we must refuse to give Satan control. Let us follow Jesus' command: *"And this gospel of the kingdom will be preached in all the world as a witness to all the nations, and then the end will come"* (Matthew 24:14).

Our goal is simple: *"The kingdoms of this world have become the kingdoms of our Lord and of His Christ, and He shall reign forever and ever!"* (Revelation 11:15).

The kingdoms of this world will become the kingdoms of

our Lord by recognizing His Lordship. As we teach His ways and proclaim His word, people will hear His voice and walk His paths.

3

Seven Mountains and The Kingdom of God

We now know that mountains are more than gigantic rocks reaching toward the sky. God uses them to establish His rule. Satan tried (and failed) to use one to establish his rule. And they are great for catching arks. Further, the Seven Mountains of Culture represent the kingdoms of this world—the places where God seeks to establish His authority. So what is our part in establishing God's kingdom on the seven mountains? What drives us to take the Seven Mountains? Who says it's our job anyway?

Well…God says.

The mandate to enforce God's authority on earth is found from Genesis to Revelation. In the beginning, God commanded Adam and Eve: *"Fill the earth and subdue it!"* (Genesis 1:28). Jesus echoed this command: *"Therefore go and make disciples of all nations,"* (Matthew 28:19). John tells us: *"And have made us kings and priests to our God; and we shall reign on the earth."* (Revelation 5: 10). And finally: *"He [Jesus] shall reign forever and ever!"* (Revelation 11:15).

This is the Kingdom commission—the Seven Mountain Mandate. It is *our* commission.

As followers of the King, we are to bring His Kingdom to the whole world, including all areas of culture. Fortunately, most of us are already active in one or more of the Seven Mountains: family, education, religion, government, business, media, or art/entertainment. The challenge, therefore, is to preach this Gospel of the Kingdom so the kingdoms of this world become the kingdoms of our Lord. To do this effectively, we have to know a little about the Gospel of the Kingdom.

The Kingdom of Heaven

The Gospel of the Kingdom….a.k.a. *The Kingdom Message*, was given to us when Jesus taught us to pray: *"Your Kingdom come. Your will be done on earth as it is in heaven"* (Matthew 6:10).

Starting with the basics, Webster defines "kingdom" as:

1. a politically organized community or major territorial unit having a monarchical form of government headed by a king,

2. a realm or region in which something is dominant; an area or sphere in which one holds a preeminent position.

The first definition is obvious: *A kingdom is a nation ruled by a king* (obviously). The secondary definition is more interesting: *Anything governed by a ruling force.*

Essentially, a kingdom is where someone or something rules the environment.

Historically, kings have claimed territory from each other and fought bloody wars for it, thinking the winner—the guy with the most soldiers left—was the real power in the disputed territories. Unfortunate for them, the ruler of a kingdom is not the potentate with a proliferation of platoons, but the leader whose voice is heard and obeyed. The true king with ruling influence is he whose word is law. (Sound familiar?) He is the true winner of any conflict and the leader of the people.

History abounds with sovereigns who did not fathom this principle.

In our history, England's King George III claimed the American colonies as part of his kingdom. To his surprise, the colonists refused to accept his words as law. Instead, they established a new kingdom where democracy determined who ruled.

Mexico refused to accept both Spain's King Ferdinand VII and later France's Emperor Napoleon III. Mexico created a new kingdom where neither Ferdinand's nor Napoleon's word was law. France also overthrew its King, disregarding his words to the point where they removed his head. Few royal edicts were uttered after that.

Revolutions often start from within a country or ruled territory when the common people start listening to a voice other than the proclaimed leader. Discontent, agitation, and finally insurrection are fomented through the influence of new and emerging leaders who, if successful, assume power in place of the fallen governing body whose words no long influence the people.

Fundamentally, a kingdom is established around a controlling influence: a person (a king, queen, bishop or pope), a form of government (democracy, communism, humanism), or a core belief system (Protestantism, Catholicism, Calvinism). Whatever has the controlling influence—whose word is *obeyed*—is the king of that realm.

Even a people-group can be a kingdom. My first career was as a systems engineer in the late 70's. I helped pioneer the early generation of digital computers. As such, I belonged to the engineering culture—part of the business mountain. We had our own language (some good, some not-so-good), our own peculiar behaviors, social norms, special knowledge, and nerd-driven humor. For example: *"There are 10 types of people in the world. Those who understand binary and those who don't."* (We could have gone on the road.)

All those things formed a culture—the kingdom of engineering. Because it was primarily influenced by technology, technology was our king.

The king can also be a philosophy. Today's education system is controlled primarily by the philosophy of humanism. Therefore, humanism is the king of education.

Obviously, the Seven Mountains metaphor cannot explain all of culture, but the principle of influence is clear. Every, nation, people, sphere—every *kingdom*—has a controlling influence that directs its operation, be it for good, evil, or somewhere in between. Our mission is to bring God's influence into every kingdom of this world, conforming them to godliness and making each the Kingdom of our Lord as they learn to hear and obey His word.

When Jesus said, *"this gospel of the kingdom* will be preached in all *the* world"* (Matthew 24:14), He meant for us to bring the influence of God into every people and culture.

I find this interpretation of the Kingdom Message liberating because it gives us the opportunity to express the Kingdom of God wherever we are found. I can build the Kingdom on whatever mountain I find myself.

Yet, despite my newfound liberty, there is still an important step to take. We must be sure our understanding of the kingdom can be biblically supported.

The Gospel of the Kingdom

The New Testament begins and ends with the Kingdom. The Kingdom was Jesus' central message while He was on the earth. Indeed, the Gospels contain more kingdom references than the rest of the New Testament. Matthew alone has 55 verses about the Kingdom, more than any other book in the Bible. Luke is second with 44; then Mark with 19; and finally John with 2 Kingdom verses.

Since Matthew dominates in kingdom verses, let's examine it closely for a clearer understanding of the Gospel of the Kingdom.

The Kingdom is first announced by John the Baptist

In those days John the Baptist came into the wilderness of Judea proclaiming, "Repent, for the kingdom of heaven is near.

Matthew 3:1-2

While most students of the gospel focus on John's message of repentance, we see here that John's purpose in calling for repentance is related to the impending Kingdom. Like the camel hair-clad prophet himself, the Gospel of Salvation is only the precursor to the Gospel of the Kingdom. Yes, repentance and salvation are necessary to enter the Kingdom, but the Kingdom itself is the real goal.

Immediately after Jesus' baptism and temptations, we see that Jesus has a different agenda: *"preaching the gospel of the kingdom"* (Matthew 4:23). Jesus tells His disciples to do likewise in Matthew

10. Finally, in Matthew 24, all believers are all commissioned to preach the Gospel of the Kingdom to the whole world.

> *From that time Jesus began to preach and to say, "Repent, for <u>the kingdom of heaven</u> is at hand."*
>
> Matthew 4:17
>
> *And Jesus went about all Galilee, teaching in their synagogues, <u>preaching the gospel of the kingdom</u>, and healing all kinds of sickness and all kinds of disease among the people.*
>
> Matthew 4:23
>
> *Then Jesus went about all the cities and villages, teaching in their synagogues, <u>preaching the gospel of the kingdom</u>, and healing every sickness and every disease among the people.*
>
> Matthew 9:35
>
> *And as you go, preach, saying, "The <u>kingdom of heaven</u> is at hand."*
>
> Matthew 10:7
>
> *And this <u>gospel of the kingdom</u> will be preached in all the world as a witness to all the nations, and then the end will come.*
>
> Matthew 24:14

In spite of all this teaching, the disciples struggled to understand the kingdom message. Late in their relationship with Jesus, they were still expecting Jesus to establish a natural Kingdom in Israel, perhaps with one or more of them appointed co-kings!

> *At that time the disciples came to Jesus, saying, "Who*

then is greatest in the kingdom of heaven?"

Matthew 18:1

And He said to her, "What do you wish?" She said to Him, "Grant that these two sons of mine may sit, one on Your right hand and the other on the left, in Your kingdom."

Matthew 20:21

Frankly, I don't know how Jesus kept His temper. All that time and they still weren't getting it. Even after Jesus' death and resurrection, the disciples still misunderstood the Kingdom:

"Therefore, when they had come together, they asked Him, saying, "Lord, will You at this time restore the kingdom to Israel?"

Acts 1:6

Maybe they should have read this book? Just a thought…

A Working Definition of the Kingdom of God

While Matthew, Mark, and Luke give significant place to Jesus' kingdom message, they contain no clear definition of the Kingdom. They have many teachings about the *qualities* of the kingdom. They have descriptions of the *type of people* that will enter the kingdom. They even have *illustrations* about how the kingdom should work. But they have no definition.

Thank God for the book of John. While it only has two passages that directly refer to the kingdom, both are home runs.

John 3 famously deals with salvation as the necessary condition to entering the Kingdom:

Jesus answered and said to him, "Most assuredly, I

say to you, unless one is born again, he cannot see
the kingdom of God." Nicodemus said to Him, "How
can a man be born when he is old? Can he enter a
second time into his mother's womb and be born?"
Jesus answered, "Most assuredly, I say to you, unless
one is born of water and the Spirit, he cannot enter
the kingdom of God."

John 3:3-5

The second reference provides the clearest definition of the Kingdom. John 18 is the story of the arrest and trial of Jesus. The Jews arrest Jesus and interrogate Him but then they ask Pilate (the Roman magistrate) to take the case because the Jewish courts cannot invoke a death penalty. At first, Pilate refuses and returns the jurisdiction back to the Jewish court, but the Jews insist that Jesus be tried by the Romans since the charge is insurrection against the Roman government. So Pilate reluctantly takes the case and questions Jesus about the serious charge of insurrection. Of course, the key question to Pilate—a king in his own right—is whether or not Jesus claims to be the King of Israel.

Then Pilate entered the Praetorium again, called
Jesus, and said to Him, "Are You the King of the Jews?"
Jesus answered him, "Are you speaking for yourself
about this, or did others tell you this concerning Me?"
Pilate answered, "Am I a Jew? Your own nation and
the chief priests have delivered You to me. What have
You done?" Jesus answered, "My kingdom is not of
this world. If My kingdom were of this world, My
servants would fight, so that I should not be delivered
to the Jews; but now My kingdom is not from here."

*Pilate therefore said to Him, "Are You a king then?"
Jesus answered, "You say rightly that I am a king. For
this cause I was born, and for this cause I have come
into the world, that I should bear witness to the truth.
Everyone who is of the truth hears My voice."*

John 18:33-35

The interplay in this exchange is marvelous, were it not the precursor to our Lord's agonizing death.

Pilate is a busy man and so gets right to the core issue: *"Are you the king of the Jews?"*

Jesus first challenges the evidence and jurisdiction by questioning why Pilate is asking him about being a king: *"Are you speaking for yourself about this, or did others tell you this concerning Me?"*

Pilate seems taken aback by Jesus' challenge and reacts defensively: *"Am I a Jew?"* Pilate follows up in a way that admits he has no evidence: *"Your own nation and the chief priests have delivered You to me."* Then Pilate retreats to an open-ended question, *"What have you done?"* It sounds as if he is ready to end the interrogation.

Jesus' answer reopens the king question but in an indirect way. Jesus explains that *"my kingdom is not of this world,"* implying He is a king. However, He denies the charge of insurrection and, as proof, points out that His servants are not fighting for Him. This is a direct answer to the charge of insurrection and rebellion, but Pilate is confused by Jesus' answer and asks again, *"Are you a king then?"*

Jesus' final answer nails it:

"You say rightly that I am a king. For this cause I was

born, and for this cause I have come into the world,
that I should bear witness to the truth. Everyone who
is of the truth hears My voice."

Jesus was born to be a king. His purpose as a king is to *"bear witness to the truth."* His concluding statement, however, establishes His kingdom. His is a kingdom of truth, and those *of* the truth— His followers—are those who hear His voice.

Jesus is defining His kingdom as one where citizens *hear* His voice. This is very similar to our dictionary definition: A kingdom is where a king's word is law. Jesus is saying His kingdom is not a geographical or political place such as Rome; rather, His Kingdom is *wherever someone hears His voice.*

Ironically, few people then, as today, heard the voice that identifies the essence of His Kingdom. So let me be clear, echoing Jesus' words.

To join the Kingdom of God, you must hear His voice.

The definition seems too simple. It can't be that easy, can it?

4

Jesus—Hear Him

Like many of us, Jesus liked to get away to the mountains. The marked difference, however, was what transpired after He got there. In Luke 9, we read of the Mount of Transfiguration. In this story, Jesus has recently empowered His 12 disciples and sent them to preach the Kingdom of God (Luke 9:2), then fed five thousand hungry people who had assembled to hear him preach. Now Jesus is going to slip away, and He's taking His three closest disciples with Him.

> *28 Now it came to pass, about eight days after these sayings, that He took Peter, John, and James and went up on the mountain to pray. 29 As He prayed, the appearance of His face was altered, and His robe became white and glistening. 30 And behold, two men talked with Him, who were Moses and Elijah, 31 who appeared in glory and spoke of His decease which He was about to accomplish at Jerusalem. 32 But Peter and those with him were heavy with sleep; and when they were fully awake, they saw His glory and the two men who stood with Him. 33 Then it happened, as*

they were parting from Him, that Peter said to Jesus, "Master, it is good for us to be here; and let us make three tabernacles: one for You, one for Moses, and one for Elijah"—not knowing what he said. ³⁴ While he was saying this, a cloud came and overshadowed them; and they were fearful as they entered the cloud. ³⁵ And a voice came out of the cloud, saying, "This is My beloved Son. Hear Him!" ³⁶ When the voice had ceased, Jesus was found alone. But they kept quiet, and told no one in those days any of the things they had seen.

Luke 9:28-35

This is an amazing story. Aside from the fact that He converses with dead people, Jesus seems to be transformed before Moses and Elijah appear. Incredibly, the disciples almost sleep through it! Finally, God caps things off by speaking from a cloud that overshadows them.

Considering that these are the only three times in Jesus' life that the Father speaks audibly, each time must be significant.

God first spoke over Jesus at His baptism:

And the Holy Spirit descended in bodily form like a dove upon Him, and a voice came from heaven which said, "You are My beloved Son; in You I am well pleased."

Luke 3:22

This is the Father speaking personally to Jesus, conveying His love and acceptance.

The second time God spoke, Jesus was talking in public to His disciples about the purpose of His impending death

> *"Now My soul is troubled, and what shall I say? 'Father, save Me from this hour'? But for this purpose I came to this hour. Father, glorify Your name." Then a voice came from heaven, saying, "I have both glorified it and will glorify it again."*

John 12:27-28

However, on the Mount of Transfiguration, the Father doesn't speak to Jesus; rather, He addresses the three disciples. In fact, this is the only time recorded that God's audible voice will be directed at them. We know this was impactful because when Peter refers to this event later, he doesn't mention the glowing Jesus, or Moses and Elijah. He only talks about God's voice.

> *"For He received from God the Father honor and glory when such a voice came to Him from the Excellent Glory: 'This is My beloved Son, in whom I am well pleased.' And we heard this voice which came from heaven when we were with Him on the holy mountain."*

2 Peter 1:17-18

So what was impactful about these words? I mean…*other* than hearing the Holy God speak from a cloud as the Son of God shines with eternal glory in the presence of Old Testament patriarchs? Given the importance of this event, I would expect a profound statement from the Father. But all God says is, *"This is My beloved Son. Hear Him!"*

Hear Him?

The first part of the statement is important but already well known. *Yes God, we get it. He's your son and you love Him.* No, if there is something important here, it has to be the latter phrase: *"hear Him."*

Please don't miss this just as the three disciples nearly did. The most important instruction given to us from that mountaintop experience is to *"hear Him."* Now, I know what you're thinking: *How can you NOT hear Him when standing beside him atop a mountain?* Somehow, I think the Father was getting at something more lasting than the immediate situation. It sounds a lot like Jesus describing the Kingdom of God to Pilate. *"Everyone who is of the truth <u>hears My voice</u>"* (John 18:37).

Of all the things the Father could have said to these shaken disciples in that supreme teachable moment: worship, pray, study, learn, walk in holiness, cleanse your life, feed the poor, take up your cross and follow Jesus…

… He simply said, *"Hear Him."*

Hear Him. Hear Jesus. But how?

The Teacher

In John chapter 16, Jesus is telling His disciples that He must leave, but He's not doing it in the usual way. Instead of "goodbye, so long, see you later," He continues a pattern of describing things they have yet to experience. Yet the only thing registering with the grief-stricken disciples is pain.

> *"But now I go away to Him who sent Me, and none of you asks Me, 'Where are You going?' But because I have said these things to you, sorrow has filled your heart.*

> John 16:5-6

Even though Jesus insists that His departure is for the best, His assurance is as unfathomable as the reasons for His impending exit.

> *Nevertheless I tell you the truth. It is to your advantage that I go away; for if I do not go away, the Helper will not come to you; but if I depart, I will send Him to you.*
>
> John 16:7

Can you imagine the thoughts of the disciples in these dark moments? *Who is this Helper? When is He coming? What will He do, exactly? And why are we capitalizing His pronouns?*

It gets worse.

Imagine the weight of shock as they digest Jesus' next words.

> *"I still have many things to say to you, but you cannot bear them now."*
>
> John 16:12

As they gather their thoughts, they must be incredulous.

So you are leaving us, Jesus, and you haven't told us everything we need to know? The Jews hate us, the Romans are wary of us, and hungry crowds seeking miracles follow us everywhere. And now YOU are leaving us, to God-knows-where, and yet you say you have more to tell us? How are you going to do that?

Fortunately for them and for us, Jesus' next words begin to unravel the mystery.

> *However, when He, the Spirit of truth, has come, He will guide you into all truth; for He will not speak on His own authority, but whatever He hears He*

will speak; and He will tell you things to come. He will glorify Me, for He will take of what is Mine and declare it to you. All things that the Father has are Mine. Therefore, I said that He will take of Mine and declare it to you.

John 16:13-15

So the "Hear Him…how?" is answered. Here's how Jesus is going to do it. The Helper: *"He will take of mine and declare it to you."* The disciples are to *"hear Him,"*—hear Jesus as the Father declared on the Mt. of Transfiguration—through the Holy Spirit. He will guide; He will tell; He will declare. He will *speak.*

It is not the nature of the Father to commission without equipping. In telling believers to *"Hear Him,"* God already planned for how we would hear—by His Spirit. But this provision is more than just an invitation to the destitute and lonely. It's an imperative to all believers.

Let's understand why.

The Kingdom to Those Who HEAR

Remarkably, Jesus' words to the Disciples—some of the last He would ever speak on Earth—establish a dichotomy of mountaintop experiences between Mt. Sinai of the Law and Mt. Zion of Grace. From Hebrews, we read:

For you have not come to the mountain [Mount Sinai] that may be touched and that burned with fire, and to blackness and darkness and tempest, and the sound of a trumpet and the voice of words, so that those who heard it begged that the word should not be spoken to them anymore.

Hebrews 12:18-20

Those hearing the law at the base of Mount Sinai could not endure the voice of God, and rightly so! They understood instinctively the gravity of their sinful situation. But now through Christ, we are able to commune freely with God. The mountain of the law has been replaced by the mountain of freedom where Jesus has mediated our way into God's presence.

> But you have come to Mount Zion and to the city of the living God, the heavenly Jerusalem, to an innumerable company of angels, to the general assembly and church of the firstborn who are registered in heaven, to God the Judge of all, to the spirits of just men made perfect, to Jesus the Mediator of the new covenant, and to the blood of sprinkling that speaks better things than that of Abel.
>
> Hebrews 12:22-24

Angels, heaven, and a new covenant! So far, so good. But things are about to get sterner. Let's continue…

> See that you do not refuse Him who speaks. For if they did not escape who refused Him who spoke on earth, much more shall we not escape if we turn away from Him who speaks from heaven, whose voice then shook the earth; but now He has promised, saying, "Yet once more I shake not only the earth, but also heaven.
>
> Hebrews 12:25-26

Just as Jesus said to Pilate, and just as the Father said to the three disciples, the phrase *"See that you do not refuse Him who speaks,"* simply means to *"hear Him."* And what happens as we hear Him?

Therefore, since we are receiving a kingdom which cannot be shaken, let us have grace, by which we may serve God acceptably with reverence and godly fear.

Hebrews 12:28

As we hear Him, we receive the unshakable Kingdom of God.

Before we can permeate the seven mountains of culture, we have to inhabit the singular mountain of God. It is there that we learn to hear Him. It is there that we receive the Kingdom of God.

And so it begins.

5

Keys of the Kingdom

As we enter into Kingdom relationship with God, preparing for the transformation of world culture, we must grasp the key principles of Kingdom living. One of those principles, found in Matthew 16, is modestly called *The Keys to The Kingdom*. It starts in one of the most celebrated passages in the New Testament as Peter reveals Jesus as the Christ.

> *When Jesus came into the region of Caesarea Philippi, He asked His disciples, saying, "Who do men say that I, the Son of Man, am?" So they said, "Some say John the Baptist, some Elijah, and others Jeremiah or one of the prophets." He said to them, "But who do you say that I am?" Simon Peter answered and said, "You are the Christ, the Son of the living God."*
>
> Matthew 16:13-16

This is arguably one of Peter's finer moments, considering what soon transpires: violence, denial, abject terror, and soul-crushing remorse. Yes, Peter learns things the hard way, but here he gets it right the first time. Jesus acknowledges as much.

Jesus answered and said to him, "Blessed are you, Simon Bar-Jonah, for flesh and blood has not revealed this to you, but My Father who is in heaven."

Matthew 16:17

Then, in one of the most widely interpreted passages in scripture, Jesus seems to convey an astounding blessing on his fledgling apostle.

"And I also say to you that you are Peter, and <u>on this rock I will build My church</u>, and the gates of Hades shall not prevail against it.

Matthew 16:18

Cool, huh? Who doesn't want to be declared the rock of Jesus' church? Especially in the hearing of the fellow disciples. Rock envy, anyone? Then, as if this isn't enough, Jesus lets loose with the ultimate decree.

"And I will give you the keys of the kingdom of heaven, and whatever you bind on earth will be bound in heaven, and whatever you loose on earth will be loosed in heaven."

Matthew 16:19

A revelation, rock-star status, and now the keys to the kingdom—things couldn't get any better for rising-star Peter, but things are not always what they seem. We need to reexamine what Jesus said in light of our growing revelation of the Kingdom and the voice of God.

Upon Further Review

The story of the Keys of the Kingdom actually begins as Jesus walks with His disciples and asks how other people see Him. The disciples answer, *"Some say John the Baptist, some Elijah, and others Jeremiah or one of the prophets."* Interestingly, everyone seems to identify Jesus as a prophet. But when Jesus then challenges the disciples directly: *"But who do you say that I am?"* Peter nails it: *"You are the Christ, the Son of the living God."*

What surprises me is how Jesus responds to Peter.

At first, Jesus seems excited, strongly affirming Peter: *"Blessed are you, Simon Bar-Jonah."* This affirmation is coupled with an explanation: *"for flesh and blood has not revealed this to you, but My Father who is in heaven."*

Jesus' excitement is evident by His sudden departure from casual conversation to the dramatic statements following, including his famous declaration *"upon this rock I will build my church."*

So what is Jesus excited about? And what rock is Jesus referring to?

I'm glad you asked.

The historical interpretation (Catholic, Anglican, Orthodox) is that Peter himself is the rock upon which Jesus will build His church. This interpretation is primarily drawn from the phrase in verse 18, *"And I also say to you that you are Peter."* Jesus declares that *Simon* (Hebrew: *Shaking Reed*) will be known as *Peter* (Greek: *Rock*). This personal reference to Peter leads the historic churches to believe the *Rock* of the church is a person, specifically Peter and his successors. This interpretation, therefore, requires the church to establish an apostolic succession to maintain the rock of the church in the current incarnation of Peter. Hence the Catholic pope, the Anglican archbishop, and the Orthodox patriarch.

Protestant churches, as you might guess, interpret the scripture differently. Rather than the *person* Peter, they say it is the *revelation* Peter received that is the *rock*. And what was that revelation? That Jesus is *"the Christ, the Son of the living God."* This, they believe, is the rock upon which Jesus will build His church.

I completely agree that this is a foundational revelation. Jesus is the Son of God! However, this revelation was not new to the disciples. Even before Simon Peter is called by Jesus to be a Fisher of Men, his brother Andrew told him that Jesus is the Messiah (John 1:41). Why then the excitement from Jesus when Peter correctly identifies Him as the Christ? (Well, it was Peter, after all.)

Yes, the revelation of Jesus as the Christ is foundational to our faith. But there has to be more to *rock* because this revelation is not actually what Jesus responds to in the scripture. Look closer. In verse 17, after Jesus blesses Simon, and before He calls him Peter, Jesus says, *"for flesh and blood has not revealed this to you, but My Father who is in heaven."* Notice that Jesus does not refer directly to what Peter said. Instead of saying, *"Peter, you are blessed because you know who I am,"* Jesus responds excitedly to the way Peter receives this revelation.

Jesus says Peter is blessed and transformed from Simon (shaking reed) to Peter (solid rock) because Peter was able to hear the voice of *"My Father who is in heaven."* The emphasis of Jesus' response to Peter is that Peter's understanding of Jesus' identity did not come from a human source. Peter did not gain this knowledge from study or observation or even from Jesus' teaching. Rather, Peter heard from the *"Father who is in heaven."*

When Peter could hear the voice of God, Jesus had a rock upon which to build His church. Yeah!

The Rock Of The Church Is The Voice Of God.

Now, don't get me wrong. I'm all for succession of leadership. And St. Peter's Basilica in Rome is gorgeous. But we have to get Jesus' teachings right. I firmly believe the rock He meant in Matthew 16 is the act of hearing God's voice and doing what God says.

In case you still need convincing, let's look at what Jesus says about himself.

> Then Jesus answered and said to them, "Most assuredly, I say to you, the Son can do nothing of Himself, but _what he sees the Father do_; for whatever he does, the Son also does in like manner."
>
> John 5:19

> "I can of myself do nothing. _As I hear, I judge;_ and my judgment is righteous, because I do not seek my own will but the will of the Father who sent me."
>
> John 5:30

In both of these passages, Jesus is identifying the means by which He does what He does. Notice the action words in these key phrases: _"what he sees the Father do,"_ and _"As I hear, I judge."_ He _sees_ the Father, He _hears_ the Father. Jesus is describing revelation as the key to his ministry.

In John 16, Jesus adds one more dimension to the revelation that His work is built on.

> "However, when he, the Spirit of truth, has come, he will guide you into all truth; for he will not speak

on his own authority, but <u>whatever he hears he will speak.</u>"

John 16:13-15

Notice that the Holy Spirit acts upon revelation as well.

In that seminal moment, surrounded by eager disciples— the foundational members of all He came to earth to establish—Jesus is saying He will build His church on the rock of *revelation.*

This means when we hear the voice of God:

- We are changed from shaking reeds (a.k.a. Simon) to solid rocks (Peter)
- We have the keys of the kingdom of heaven
- We can bind and loose on earth as it is in heaven
- The gates of Hell cannot prevail against us

In short: Our Kingdom authority is derived from our ability to hear God's voice.

Without authority, we cannot build a kingdom, but without revelation from the King, we have no authority.

And yet, it wasn't always like this.

Paradise Lost

Man was created in the image of God. He communed with God and held authority over the earth (Genesis 1). Unfortunately, man lost his God-given authority when he sinned. This much is widely known. However, the *way* man lost his authority is the essential element to understanding how man must regain his authority.

The story of original sin found in Genesis 3 begins with the serpent questioning Eve about what God has told her: *"Has God indeed said?"* Notice that the enemy's first challenge is to man's ability to hear the voice of God.

> *Now the serpent was more cunning than any beast of the field which the LORD God had made. And he said to the woman, "Has God indeed said, 'You shall not eat of every tree of the garden?" And the woman said to the serpent, "We may eat the fruit of the trees of the garden; but of the fruit of the tree which is in the midst of the garden, God has said, 'You shall not eat it, nor shall you touch it, lest you die.' Then the serpent said to the woman, 'You will not surely die. For God knows that in the day you eat of it your eyes will be opened, and you will be like God, knowing good and evil.'*

> Genesis 3:1-5

Eve's response to the serpent's challenge is weak and inaccurate. She fails to identify the tree and adds a penalty for simply touching the fruit (see Genesis 2:16). Then the serpent accuses God of lying, telling Eve *"You will not surely die."* Finally, he offers Eve a life without hearing God's voice: *"you will be like God, knowing good and evil."* Tragically, Eve falls for the deception and makes a similar offer to Adam who also falls.

Before long, the newly-minted "gods" are summoned by the voice of God and hide behind a rock.

> *And they heard the sound of the Lord God walking in the garden in the cool of the day, and Adam and his wife hid themselves from the presence of the Lord God among the trees of the garden. Then the Lord God called to Adam and said to him, "Where are you?" So*

he said, "I heard Your voice in the garden, and I was afraid because I was naked; and I hid myself."

Genesis 3:8-10

For the first time in his life, man is afraid of the voice of God: *"I heard Your voice in the garden, and I was afraid ..."*

Things go downhill from here. Man is cursed, yet his loving God explains why he must accept the penalty.

Then to Adam He said, "Because you have heeded the voice of your wife, and have eaten from the tree of which I commanded you, saying, 'You shall not eat of it': 'Cursed is the ground for your sake; In toil you shall eat of it All the days of your life."

Genesis 3:17

The curse comes not because Adam listened to his wife (sorry, guys), but because he listened to a voice *other than God.*

Paradise Regained.

Man's dominion was lost in the Garden when he began to fear the voice of God. However, Jesus Christ came to earth to *reclaim* what Satan took in the garden—*"for the Son of Man has come to seek and to save that which was lost"* (Luke 19:10).

Now we can understand why Jesus was so excited in Matthew 16:18. Peter finally received revelation from the Father in heaven. Yeah! If Peter can get it, they all can get it! One of Jesus' primary missions on earth was accomplished—restoring the voice of God to man. Today a fisherman, tomorrow the king.

Kingdom Authority

Of all Jesus did on earth, restoring the voice of God was

fundamental to returning man's authority, and without authority, there could be no kingdom. We can see throughout scripture the link between God's voice and authority.

When Jesus asked His disciples: *"Who do men say that I, the Son of Man, am?"* Jeremiah was one of the names given. Although Jesus was not Jeremiah, this mistaken identity was bestowed with honor.

Jeremiah's call by God to be a prophet is one of the clearest prophetic calls in scripture. It can be found in Jeremiah 1. Rather than quote the entire passage, allow me to identify key aspects of this well-known passage.

In Jeremiah 1:5, God says:

> *"I ordained you a prophet to the nations...for you shall go to all to whom I send you, and whatever I command you, you shall speak."*

Then in verse 10:

> *"See, I have this day set you over the nations and over the kingdoms, to root out and to pull down, to destroy and to throw down, to build and to plant."*

Of course, people get excited over this pronouncement, and why not? It's awesome to read of a prophet set with authority over nations. Go Jeremiah! But as with most things, we revel in the final product while failing to appreciate the root cause. Verse 9 of this famous chapter tells us how the prophet is to be set over the nations.

> *Then the Lord put forth his hand and touched my mouth, and the Lord said to me: "Behold, I have put My words in your mouth. See, I have this day set you*

over the nations and over the kingdoms, to root out and to pull down, to destroy and to throw down, to build and to plant."

Jeremiah 1:9-10

God put Jeremiah over the nations by putting *His words* in his mouth. The voice of God gave the prophet his power and authority.

Jesus claims the same authority.

And Jesus came and spoke to them, saying, "All authority has been given to Me in heaven and on earth."

Matthew 28:18

He then gives the church authority to establish the Kingdom of God by making disciples of every nation.

Go therefore and make disciples of all the nations, baptizing them in the name of the Father and of the Son and of the Holy Spirit, teaching them to observe all things that I have commanded you; and lo, I am with you always, even to the end of the age. Amen.

Matthew 28:19-20

Notice that Jesus gives the disciples all authority in heaven and earth by simply *speaking* it to them. Now that they can hear the voice of God, they can receive the authority of God.

Thus it remains to this day. All authority has been given to Jesus, and He has given it to us. You'd think the story is complete, wouldn't you?

Actually, the story has only started.

(For more illumination on hearing God, refer to "I Hear Voices" in the Appendix.)

6

Kingdom Authority and Culture

As the church learns to hear the voice of God, she receives authority to bring the Kingdom of God to the Seven Mountains of culture. Within these realms of influence, we are to enforce the Kingdom. Yet, what does it mean to enforce the Kingdom?

We find a clue in the words of St. Paul. In his letter to the Romans, he contrasts the law and ritual of the Old Testament with the spirit of the New Testament. It is a spirit, says Paul, characterized by: *"righteousness and peace and joy in the Holy Spirit"* (Romans 14: 17). Apparently, enforcing the Kingdom must have something to do with these three qualities: *righteousness, peace,* and *joy.*

Righteousness, which appears 95 times in the New Testament, speaks to our fundamental relationship with God. We must be in right standing with God to participate in the Kingdom (Matthew 5:20). Joy, which appears 61 times in the New Testament, speaks to the new abundant life with the Lord in His Kingdom (Colossians 1:11-13). Both are consistently described throughout scripture as positive.

Peace, however, which also appears 95 times in the New Testament, is not always positive, nor is it always peaceful. Peace is often associated with violence, war, and might. If we are to enforce the Kingdom, we must understand peace.

What is Peace?

Peace in the New Testament is referenced strongly in both positive and negative context. Negative examples include: *"Do not suppose that I have come to bring peace to the earth. I did not come to bring peace, but a sword"* (Matthew 10:3). (Also see Luke 12:51.) The futility of seeking peace is described in 1 Thessalonians 5:3, *"For when they say, "Peace and safety!" then sudden destruction comes upon them."*

Still, positive peace references abound. Jesus gives the disciples His peace in John 14:27: *"Peace I leave with you, My peace I give to you."* Jesus' purpose on earth is described in terms of peace: *"having made peace through the blood of His cross"* (Colossians 1:20). We are told to preach the gospel of peace: *"How beautiful are the feet of those who preach the gospel of peace"* (Romans 10:15). Even Father God is repeatedly referred to as the *God of Peace*. (See Romans 15:33, Romans 16:20, Philippians 4:9, I Thessalonians 5:23, Hebrews 13:20).

Although New Testament Greek only has one word that is translated "peace," the word *eirene* can carry two meanings.

- a state of tranquility, peace between individuals, i.e. harmony, concord;

- security, safety, prosperity, felicity.

Old Testament Hebrew references to peace have a simpler interpretation. There are two words that are typically translated "peace." The common word for "peace" is *charash*, meaning quiet or tranquil. For example, *"Hold your peace with me, and let me speak, then let come on me what may!"* (Job 13:13). Other translations say *"be quiet"* instead of *"hold your peace."* (I imagine a modern slang translation might say, *"shut up!"*)

The other Hebrew word translated "peace" is *shalom*. Shalom has nothing to do with quietness. Instead, it carries the second Greek meaning: health, prosperity, and safety. This word is still used in Israel as a greeting/blessing, usually translated "peace be to you."

Knowing the true meaning of *peace* determines how we enforce it. In Isaiah, we have a wonderful passage identifying Jesus as the Prince of Peace.

> *For unto us a Child is born, unto us a Son is given... and his name will be called Wonderful, Counselor, Mighty God, Everlasting Father, Prince of Peace. Of the increase of his government and peace there will be no end, upon the throne of David and over His kingdom, to order it and establish it with judgment and justice from that time forward, even forever. The zeal of the Lord of hosts will perform this.*
>
> Isaiah 9:6-7

Sounds great, doesn't it? We have the Christ-child; we have words like *"wonderful...mighty...justice and righteousness."* But wait. What is *"mighty"* doing in the description of Jesus as the *"Prince of Peace"*? What does *might* have to do with *peace*? To understand, we should examine the language preceding Isaiah's wonderful declaration of Jesus' rule.

For as in the day of Midian's defeat, you [God] have shattered the yoke that burdens them, the bar across their shoulders, the rod of their oppressor. Every warrior's boot used in battle and every garment rolled in blood will be destined for burning, will be fuel for the fire. For to us a child is born, to us a son is given, and the government will be on his shoulders.

Isaiah 9:4-6

The language here is violent: *"shattered the yoke...oppressor... warrior's boot in battle...garment rolled in blood...burning...fire."* There is some serious carnage going on here. Apparently, conflict and peace go hand in hand.

Ironically, Christians often use Isaiah 26:3 to comfort each other in times of distress: *"You will keep in perfect peace him whose mind is steadfast, because he trusts in you."* But the full passage reveals something much different than warmth and cuddles.

In that day this song will be sung in the land of Judah: We have a strong city; God makes salvation its walls and ramparts. Open the gates that the righteous nation may enter, the nation that keeps faith. You will keep in perfect peace him whose mind is steadfast, because he trusts in you. Trust in the LORD forever, for the LORD, the LORD, is the Rock eternal. He humbles those who dwell on high, he lays the lofty city low; he levels it to the ground and casts it down to the dust. Feet trample it down - the feet of the oppressed, the footsteps of the poor.

Isaiah 26:1-6

46

Isaiah's beautiful promise of peace is set against the backdrop of violent, militant language: *"a strong city...walls and ramparts... lays the lofty city low...casts it down to the dust...trample..."* The connection between the upheaval and the comfort of peace is unmistakable. Peace requires change, but change causes conflict. Everyone wants peace; few appreciate the bloody struggle to achieve it.

Zechariah was no stranger to trouble. Here's his take on peace:

> *For thus says the LORD of hosts: ...I am determined to do good to Jerusalem and to the house of Judah. Do not fear. These are the things you shall do: Speak each man the truth to his neighbor; Give judgment in your gates for truth, justice, and peace; Let none of you think evil in your heart against your neighbor; And do not love a false oath. For all these are things that I hate, "Says the LORD." Then the word of the LORD of hosts came to me, saying, "Thus says the LORD of hosts: "The fast of the fourth month, the fast of the fifth, the fast of the seventh, and the fast of the tenth, shall be joy and gladness and cheerful feasts For the house of Judah. Therefore love truth and peace."*

> Zechariah 8:14-19,

God tells us to celebrate with joy and gladness; *therefore love truth and peace.* Yet throughout the passage, God refers to Himself as the "Lord of hosts." That title comes from *Jehovah Sabaoth*, meaning *the Lord of War*. This is the same name God uses in Isaiah 9:7 when He says *"The zeal of the LORD Almighty will accomplish this."* It may seem incongruous to use the Lord of Battles to establish a throne for the Prince of Peace, but God knows that true peace (shalom) is the result of right authority being enforced.

Now, lest we think that this kind of peace was only for Old Testament days, notice that God associates Jesus' reign with David's kingdom.

> *Of the increase of His [Jesus'] government and peace there will be no end, upon the throne of David and over His kingdom, to order it and establish it with judgment and justice from that time forward, even forever. The zeal of the Lord of hosts will perform this.*
>
> Isaiah 9:7

In Acts, Jesus is referred to as the seed of David.

> *And when He had removed him, He raised up for them David as king, to whom also He gave testimony and said, "I have found David the son of Jesse, a man after My own heart, who will do all My will." From this man's seed, according to the promise, God raised up for Israel a Savior—Jesus…*
>
> Acts 13:22-23

Historically, David did more to establish peace for God's people than any other king did, but he did it through war. Through most of David's life, he fought the enemies of God and defeated them. By the time David turned over the kingdom to Solomon, there was peace on every border of Israel because David had accomplished this. David did such a good job that there continued to be peace in the land for all of Solomon's reign. Personally, I think it would have made more sense for the Prince of Peace to sit on Solomon's throne, but God placed Him on David's throne—the king who enforced the peace through war.

Shalom peace happens when right authority is enforced. David brought shalom: health, prosperity, and safety to the kingdom.

In Ephesians, Paul writes of the authority of peace

Peace breaks down walls:

> *But now in Christ Jesus you who once were far off have been brought near by the blood of Christ. For He Himself is our peace, who has made both one, and has broken down the middle wall of separation*

Ephesians 2:13-14

Peace is a bond:

> *Endeavoring to keep the unity of the Spirit in the bond of peace.*

Ephesians 4:3

Peace outfits us for war:

> *Stand therefore, having girded your waist with truth, having put on the breastplate of righteousness, and having shod your feet with the preparation of the gospel of peace.*

Ephesians 6:14-15

Note that none of these uses of peace brings to mind calmness or quietness, but they do fit nicely with *shalom*: health, safety, prosperity.

Finally, we can have no clearer declaration of true Shalom peace than in Paul's letter to the Romans: *"And the God of peace will crush Satan under your feet shortly"* (Romans 16:20). Let that sink in for a moment. *The God of peace…does what? He crushes.* Yes, He does!

- Jesus came *"that He might destroy the works of the devil"* (1 John 3:8).

- When He heals us He *crushes* disease under our feet.

- When He provides for us, He *crushes* poverty under our feet.

- When He protects us, He *crushes* insecurity and oppression under our feet.

The Prince of Peace sits on a warrior's throne to enforce righteousness in His Kingdom. He destroys the enemy to bring *shalom*: health, safety, and prosperity to His people.

I believe *shalom* peace is desired in every culture. I mean… who doesn't want health, safety, and prosperity? This is why we have peace officers. When the peace of our home or community is threatened, we call for the peace officers to come and restore the peace. However, these peace officers do not come calmly. If our safety, health, or prosperity is under attack, we are not interested in calmness or tranquility. We want enforcement! The peace officers arrive with flashing lights and loud sirens (no calmness here). They are militant in their uniforms, badges, weapons, and restraints. We expect them to apprehend perpetrators, tackling them, binding them, and even shooting them if necessary. All this force is required to enforce the peace. Peace officers are not the lawmakers or even the judges. Rather, their job is to enforce the laws and judgments already given.

The enemy of our peace has come to kill, steal, and destroy, but our Prince of Peace has given us all power over the enemy. Just as a peace officer may declare, "Stop, in the name of the Law!" we can declare, "Stop, in the name of Jesus!"

God wants to be the Prince of Peace to us. He wants to enforce the peace—the authority of God. The church has authority to establish the peace of the Kingdom. Peace comes where God's word is law—where His voice is heard. It is our mandate to bring the Kingdom to the Seven Mountains of Culture. So let us not miss what is actually required of us. In the Kingdom, the *righteous* enforce *peace* to bring *joy*.

7

Kingdom Reformation

The Kingdom message is a transformative message that changes lives, churches, and cultures. It is not a fad diet, a get-rich-quick scheme, or a news break with film at 11. It is not here to comfort us or exalt us. It is here to bring righteousness, peace, and joy to the Seven Mountains of culture. It effects everlasting change to the glory of God.

Yes, we are in a special time of reformation; God is calling us to establish His kingdom. Now! Today! But to transform the seven mountains of culture to the kingdoms of our Lord, Christians must first be transformed individually and corporately. We must be reformed to be reformers. We must undergo reformation.

What is Reformation?

Generally, a reformation reforms an institution or practice, although when the Kingdom of God is involved, things get a bit more specific. The word "reformation" is only used once in the New Testament.

In speaking of the changes brought about by Christianity, we read in Hebrews:

"Even the first covenant had ordinances of divine service and the earthly sanctuary. For a tabernacle was prepared...the high priest went alone once a year, not without blood, which he offered for himself and for the people's sins committed in ignorance; the Holy Spirit indicating this, that the way into the Holiest of All was not yet made manifest while the first tabernacle was still standing. It was symbolic for the present time in which both gifts and sacrifices are offered which cannot make him who performed the service perfect in regard to the conscience - concerned only with foods and drinks, various washings, and fleshly ordinances imposed until <u>the time of reformation</u>.

Hebrews 9:1-5

"Reformation" comes from the Greek *diorthosis,* meaning: "a making straight" (*dia,* "through," *orthos,* "straight;"). It denotes a reforming. The word has the meaning either:

a) of a right arrangement, right ordering, or, more usually

b) of restoration, amendment, bringing right again; what is indicated here is a time when the imperfect, the inadequate, would be superseded by a better order of things (Vine's).

The dictionary definition of "reform" is:

1. a) to put or change into an improved form or condition

   b) to amend or improve by change of form or removal of faults or abuses;

2. to put an end to by enforcing or introducing a better method or course of action.

Hebrews 9:10 uses *reformation* to emphasize that Christ "made straight" the way to God when He died on the cross and rose again. Indeed, Jesus brought the most important reformation in history. And it continues today despite the many successes and failures throughout the church's progression.

To appreciate reformation and our role in it, we must examine the history of reformation, understanding what transpired in these times of upheaval that propelled the church forward. Although there are many revivals in history, we will focus on three major reformations.

The first reformation was when Jesus came to earth. The second reformation was the protestant reformation, starting in 16th century Germany. The third reformation is today.

Join me for a brief discussion of Reformation 101.

Reformations

As we review the historical and spiritual climate during times of reformation, we find several common conditions present in each reformation. We can categorize these conditions as revelation, activation, technology, and economics.

- <u>Revelation</u> is the reformed theology, that is, how we understand God.

- <u>Activation</u> is the reformed practice of the church, that is, how we relate to God.

- <u>Technology</u> is the physical capabilities available to God's people.

- <u>Economics</u> is the financial environment the church operates in.

The First Reformation

The First Reformation occurred when Jesus lived on earth and sent the Holy Spirit to establish His Kingdom.

Historical Context

In 63 BC, the Roman general Pompey conquered Jerusalem and made the Jewish kingdom a client of Rome. In 40–39 BC, Herod the Great was appointed King of the Jews by the Roman Senate, and in 6 AC, the last ethnarch of Judea was deposed by the emperor Augustus and his territories were combined with Idumea and Samaria and annexed as Iudaea Province under direct Roman administration.

Now, what did this first reformation look like?

Revelation

Theology underwent a radical transformation as Christianity emerged from Judaism, proclaiming Jesus Christ as the Son of God and the King of the Kingdom of God.

Activation

The Holy Spirit began speaking to the church, empowering it to operate as God's ambassadors to establish His Kingdom. *"On earth as it is in heaven"* became the stated goal.

Technology

Because of Pax Romana (Roman peace), the world was relatively stable. Commerce, economics, the arts, and architecture flourished amidst the political stability afforded through Roman rule. Unlike former times, this peace lasted a long time, greatly facilitating travel and communication.

Therefore, the disciples were able to travel far and wide carrying the word of God.

Economics

This is less clear, but we know Jesus' birthplace was dictated by a tax decree. The imagery on coins took an important step when Julius Caesar issued coins bearing his own portrait. In 27 BC, the Roman Republic came to an end as Augustus (63 BC–14 AD) ascended to the throne as the first emperor. Taking autocratic power, it soon became recognized that there was a link between the emperor's sovereignty and the production of coinage.

Summary

The first reformation brought us Jesus, the Holy Spirit, and the fledgling Christian church emerging from, but quickly distancing itself from, Judaism.

The Second Reformation

The 2nd Reformation occurred when Martin Luther nailed 95 theses to All Saints Church door in Wittenberg, Germany, on All Saints Day 1517. His act was a challenge to debate, calling into question much of what the Catholic church believed and practiced in that day.

Historical Context

The Protestant Reformation was the 16th-century schism within Western Christianity initiated by Martin Luther, John Calvin and other early Protestants. It was sparked by the 1517 posting of Luther's 95 Theses. The efforts of the reformers, who objected to (protested) the doctrines, rituals, and ecclesiastical structure of the Roman Catholic Church, led to the creation of new national Protestant churches. The Reformation was precipitated by earlier events within Europe, such as the Black Death and the Western Schism. Over the course of almost a century, three different men claimed to be Pope, often simultaneously. This eroded people's faith in the Catholic Church and the Papacy which governed it. This, as well as many other factors, such as the mid-15th-century invention of the printing press, the fall of the Eastern Roman Empire, the end of the Middle Ages, and the beginning of the modern era, contributed to the creation of Protestantism as we know it today.

Here is what the 2nd reformation looked like.

Revelation

The theology of the Reformers departed from the Roman Catholic Church primarily on the basis of three major principles:

- Sole authority of Scripture
- Justification by faith alone
- Priesthood of the believer.

While these ideas may not seem radical today, their effect in Luther's time was to strip power from the Catholic Church, robbing the religious hierarchy of its ability to rule over people. It brought the clergy down to earth…rapidly. Some might even say *crashingly*.

Activation

Through the priesthood of all believers, the protestant

reformation placed responsibility for relationship with God, including salvation, with individuals. No longer could the church claim to stand between God and man.

Technology

Through the invention of the printing press by Johann Gutenberg in 1439, the word of God was finally available to the common man, making the second reformation a triumph of literacy and education. Luther's translation of the Bible into German was a decisive moment in the spread of literacy and stimulated as well the printing and distribution of many other religious books and pamphlets. From 1517 onward, religious pamphlets flooded Germany and much of Europe. By 1530, over 10,000 publications were known, with a total of ten million copies. The Reformation was thus a media revolution as well as a theological revolution.

Economy

Economies reformed from a Feudal system to a Capitalist system. Feudalism took place mostly in Europe and lasted from the medieval period up through the 16th century. Feudal manors were almost entirely self-sufficient and therefore limited the role of the free market. This stifled the growth of capitalism.

However, the sudden emergence of new technologies and discoveries, particularly in the industries of agriculture and exploration, revitalized the growth of capitalism. The most important development at the end of Feudalism was the emergence of "the dichotomy between wage earners and capitalist merchants." With mercantilism, the competitive nature meant there were always winners and losers, and this was clearly evident as feudalism transitioned into mercantilism—an economic system characterized by private or corporate ownership of capital goods, by investments that are determined by private decision, and by prices, production, and the distribution of goods that are determined mainly by competition in a free market leading to the industrial revolution.

Summary

The Protestant Reformation empowered individuals by breaking the yoke of oppression fostered through ignorance and overbearing institutions—mainly the church and the economic systems of the time.

The Third Reformation

The Third Reformation is now. It is the Gospel of the Kingdom. The King is here and we must hear His voice. It declares obedience to the King through spiritual submission and social service. The Church is engaging the Seven Mountains of world culture to effect transformation, fostering the greatest revival in history.

Historical Context

We do not yet have the advantage of historical analysis; instead, we are living our history. Still, we can get a sense of what is happening. Globally, colonialism is finished. The major powers of the world: European, American, Russian, Chinese, can no longer spread their influence by expanding their territories. Attempts to do so are being met with the firm resolve of world powers committed to the freedom of nations. Democratic independent states are the norm, replacing centralized forms of government. Where dictators or oligarchs still hold power, their rule is eroding and being replaced by more democratic institutions. As the world unites, multinational organizations are growing in power and influence, among these: United Nations, World Trade Organization, European Union, NAFTA, NATO, African Union, OPEC, ASEAN, and the International Monetary Fund.

Revelation

Every saint is a minister of the Kingdom of God, as typified by "the saint's movement." The Kingdom of God is understood as relevant to our common lives. Individual relationships with God is the norm, leading to a decentralization of power as each believer learns to hear from God, acts in the authority that His voice brings, and contributes to the Church that Jesus came to establish. We are the Church.

Activation

The church is establishing the Kingdom of God through a spiritual transformation of its people and a cultural transformation of the world.

Technology

We live in unprecedented times of freedom and power—the Information Age—characterized by the ability of individuals to transfer information freely and have instant access to information that would have been impossible to reach 20 years ago. We are experiencing a shift from the traditional industrial model of the industrial revolution to an economy based on the flow of information. We are becoming an information society.

Economics

Our economies are becoming global, relying on economic interdependence of national economies across the world through a rapid increase in cross-border movement of goods, service, technology and capital.

Summary

Throughout history, reformations and the revivals that accompanied them have waxed and waned, rising on the strength of leaders and falling on the endemic faults of the same. Through this process, the aftermath of every spiritual awakening has revealed the need for greater reformation within ourselves before the next reformation can begin. Our quest to bring the Kingdom of God to the Seven Mountains of culture must begin where Jesus said:

> *"The kingdom of God does not come with observation; nor will they say, 'See here!' or 'See there! For indeed, the kingdom of God is within you."*

> Luke 17: 20-21

Likewise, theologies that would have us address the transformation of world cultures primarily from a political aspect miss Jesus' answer to this very issue.

> *"Jesus answered, 'My kingdom is not of this world. If My kingdom were of this world, My servants would fight, so that I should not be delivered to the Jews; but now My kingdom is not from here."*

> John 18:36

Clearly, Jesus is not leading a political social action movement.

Rather, He is establishing a kingdom that transforms lives to change society.

The Kingdom Message

The Third Reformation establishes the Kingdom of God within our cultures, proclaiming the kingdom message that began when Jesus proclaimed His ministry on earth from Isaiah 61:

> *So He came to Nazareth, where He had been brought up. And as His custom was, He went into the synagogue on the Sabbath day, and stood up to read. And He was handed the book of the prophet Isaiah. And when He had opened the book, He found the place where it was written: "The Spirit of the LORD is upon Me, Because He has anointed Me to preach the gospel to the poor; He has sent Me to heal the brokenhearted, to proclaim liberty to the captives and recovery of sight to the blind, to set at liberty those who are oppressed; to proclaim the acceptable year of the LORD."*
>
> Luke 4:16-19

The phrase *"to proclaim the acceptable year of the LORD"* is from Isaiah 61:2, a direct reference to the Sabbath year of Jubilee—the great 50th year festival of the Hebrews when the land was to rest and the Israelites were only permitted to gather the spontaneous produce of the fields (Leviticus 25:11-12). All inherited property reverted to its original family ownership (Leviticus 25:13-34; Leviticus 27:16-24). All who were slaves were set free (Leviticus 25:39-54) and all debts were cancelled. In return, God so blessed the land that it brought forth enough for the Sabbath years (Leviticus 25:20-22).

The key elements of the Jubilee, and therefore the Kingdom Message, are:

- provision
- favor
- freedom
- healing

These are reflected in the proclamation of Isaiah 61 which is in turn incorporated into Jesus' declaration of His ministry on earth.

> *The Spirit of the Lord God is upon Me,*
>
> *Because the Lord has anointed Me*
>
> *To preach good tidings to the poor;*
>
> *He has sent Me to heal the brokenhearted,*
>
> *To proclaim liberty to the captives,*
>
> *And the opening of the prison to those who are bound;*
>
> *To proclaim the acceptable year of the Lord,*
>
> *And the day of vengeance of our God;*
>
> *To comfort all who mourn,*
>
> *To console those who mourn in Zion,*
>
> *To give them beauty for ashes,*
>
> *The oil of joy for mourning,*
>
> *The garment of praise for the spirit of heaviness;*
>
> *That they may be called trees of righteousness,*
>
> *The planting of the Lord, that He may be glorified."*
>
> Isaiah 61:1-3

Spiritual vs. Natural

Bible teachers often mistake these key elements of the Kingdom as exclusively spiritual. Following this interpretation, Jesus, in His declaration that initiated the Kingdom message, must have meant the *spiritually* poor, *spiritually* captive, *spiritually* blind, and *spiritually* oppressed. A closer examination, however, reveals a greater truth.

The tendency to interpret scripture in a purely spiritual way is referred to as a "pre-restoration" by Dr. Bill Hamon. In his book *Prophets and the Prophetic Movement*, Dr. Hamon describes seven characteristics of a restoration movement. One of the characteristics is that restored revelation becomes manifest in the *natural world* rather than reserved to a *spiritual reality only*. Further, the restored revelation becomes available commonly rather than restricted to special individuals or groups.

For example, the Second Reformation restored the priesthood of the believer and the understanding of personal salvation by faith and grace. This restored revelation allowed the common believer to go boldly before the throne of grace, a place previously thought accessible only to church-ordained priests and high officials.

From a *restoration* view of Jesus' proclamation in Luke 4:18, we can accept the spiritual interpretation as well as a physical interpretation and understand what the Kingdom Message entails.

- "Good news to the poor" can mean freedom from poverty
- "Release to the captives" can mean release from all kinds of bondage
- "Restoring sight to the blind" can mean physical healing
- "Freedom to the oppressed" can mean transformation to our culture and society

What a richer understanding of the favor of the Lord! We see a similar set of elements when Jesus teaches the disciples to pray.

In this manner, therefore, pray: Our Father in heaven, Hallowed be Your name. Your kingdom come. Your will be done on earth as it is in heaven. Give us this day our daily bread. And forgive us our debts, as we forgive our debtors. And do not lead us into temptation, but deliver us from the evil one. For Yours is the kingdom and the power and the glory forever. Amen.

Matthew 6: 9-13

While the prayer begins and ends with the Kingdom, notice a dual emphasis including the more spiritual issues such as: *"do not lead us into temptation"* and *"deliver us from the evil one."* These are spoken alongside natural issues such as *"give us our daily bread"* and *"forgive us our debts."* In teaching us to pray, Jesus identifies spiritual and natural elements for the coming Kingdom in which the Father's will is done *"on earth as it is in heaven."*

Sheep and Goat Nations

In addition to a clearer understanding of spiritual and natural, we have a striking connection between the Kingdom and natural action from the gospel of Matthew:

"When the Son of Man comes in His glory, and all the holy angels with Him, then He will sit on the throne of His glory. All the nations will be gathered before Him, and He will separate them one from another, as a shepherd divides his sheep from the goats. And He will set the sheep on His right hand, but the goats on the left. Then the King will say to those on His right hand, 'Come, you blessed of My Father, inherit the

kingdom prepared for you from the foundation of the world: for I was hungry and you gave Me food; I was thirsty and you gave Me drink; I was a stranger and you took Me in; I was naked and you clothed Me; I was sick and you visited Me; I was in prison and you came to Me."

Matthew 25:31-40

Notice the physical criteria the King uses to judge nations. It is based on their treatment of those who are hungry, thirsty, alien, naked, sick, and imprisoned. Those who care for such are called the "sheep nations"—followers of the King. Curiously, there is no mention of any spiritual requirements or activity: no evangelism, speaking in tongues, miracles, nor gifts of the Spirit. In fact, the sheep nations are referred to as the righteous: *"Then the righteous will answer Him"* (v37). Jesus then ties their good works directly to Himself: *"And the King will answer and say to them, 'Assuredly, I say to you, inasmuch as you did it to one of the least of these My brethren, you did it to Me'"* (v40).

This is echoed in James 2:5, *"Listen, my beloved brethren: Has God not chosen the poor of this world to be rich in faith and heirs of the kingdom which He promised to those who love Him?"*

Of course, we must balance this with scriptures declaring the spiritual requirements for entering the Kingdom:

Do you not know that the unrighteous will not inherit the kingdom of God,

1 Corinthians 6:9

Now this I say, brethren, that flesh and blood cannot inherit the kingdom of God; nor does corruption inherit incorruption,

1 Corinthians 15:50

Envy, murders, drunkenness, revelries, and the like; of which I tell you beforehand, just as I also told you in time past, that those who practice such things will not inherit the kingdom of God

Galatians 5:21

"Most assuredly, I say to you, unless one is born again, he cannot see the kingdom of God."

John 3:3

For this you know, that no fornicator, unclean person, nor covetous man, who is an idolater, has any inheritance in the kingdom of Christ and God.

Ephesians 5:5

As these scriptures indicate, there are two aspects to the Kingdom of God. First, there is the spiritual requirement that you must be born again and live righteously. Second, there is a natural requirement to minister to the needs around us. I see the church falling into two general groups, each emphasizing one of these Kingdom aspects. Typically, the Pentecostal, Charismatic and other more theologically conservative evangelical churches focus on the spiritual needs: salvation, spiritual baptism, healing, deliverance, discipleship. On the other hand, more theologically liberal churches focus on social action: feeding the poor, building hospitals, reaching the homeless. The Third Reformation brings a full Gospel of the Kingdom that recombines these functions, enabling us to bring spiritual transformation *and* social transformation to our culture.

And this gospel of the kingdom will be preached in <u>all</u> <u>the world</u> as a witness to all the nations, and then the end will come.

Matthew 24:14

Go therefore and make disciples of all the nations.

Matthew 28:19

God establishes the perfect balance. He sends reformation to prepare the way for the coming of the Lord. He comes spiritually to every believer and will come physically to the whole world.

We are each called to impact the sphere of influence to which God has called us. As each of us hears His voice, we reclaim the culture one person at a time, one industry at a time, one mountain at a time. The kingdoms of this world become the kingdoms of our Lord, both physically and spiritually.

8

Times of Awakening

The greatest revival the world has ever seen is coming, heralding the arrival of our Lord. We are seeing the fulfillment of Paul's words to the Romans: *"As surely as I live," says the Lord, "every knee will bow before me; every tongue will acknowledge God"* (Romans 14:11). Knees are bowing. All of creation is coming under the lordship of Jesus Christ. The Seven Mountains of Culture are awakening to the light of God.

Someday, historians will name a person, place, and time for the official beginning of this present reformation just as they did for the Second Reformation (Martin Luther, Wittenberg Germany, October 31, 1517). That's just what historians do. However, the Third Reformation is not about a point in history. Rather, it is the culmination of a move of the Spirit of God over many people, places and times.

The spiritual actions that contribute to the overall reformation carry various names: revival, refreshing, renewal, restoration, movement, and awakening. They occur in many venues, from single congregations to communities to international movements; everywhere that people hear the voice of God. Some are never reported beyond their own circles while others get worldwide exposure. Some are brief while others continue for decades. Each is a response to God moving in the earth to accomplish His purpose.

The Awakening

The events called "Awakening" have a cherished meaning for the church in the United States since there were three "great awakenings" that contributed to the formation of our nation and its early development. While some of these awakenings were primarily USA events, others had a global impact and implications. The history of awakenings in America can be illustrative of the worldwide reformation we are experiencing today.

A brief review of these awakenings shows an interesting pattern. Throughout history, there has been an awakening event every 50 to 60 years. Starting in 1730-1741, we see subsequent awakenings in 1800-1804, 1857-1859, 1906-1909, 1960-1967. This equates to every other generation, meaning the young people of one event would be the grandparents in the next event. If this pattern holds true, the USA is due for a new awakening in the 2010's.

It is vital that we understanding awakenings and their influence on society and, more importantly, on the Church. The next few paragraphs are a bit historical but please stay with me as we follow this path of discovery and understand the Church of today.

The First Great Awakening 1730-1741

The First Great Awakening was driven by leaders such as Johnathan Edwards, John Wesley, and George Whitefield. While there is not much evidence that great institutions were formed, or even any special movements created, it is clear that the generation most influenced by this awakening is the generation that established America's independence from Great Britain. The First Great Awakening affected the grandparents and parents of the generation that declared independence as a right bestowed by their Creator.

> *We hold these truths to be self-evident, that all men are created equal, that they are endowed by their Creator with certain unalienable Rights, that among these are Life, Liberty and the pursuit of Happiness.*
>
> Declaration of Independence, July 4, 1776

The Second Great Awakening 1800-1804

Charles Finney was a well-known leader in the Second Great Awakening. In the midst of shifts in theology and church polity, American Christians took it upon themselves to reform society during this period. Known commonly as antebellum reform, this phenomenon included reforms in temperance, womens' rights, abolitionism, and a multitude of other questions faced by society. The religious enthusiasm of the Second Great Awakening was echoed by the new political enthusiasm of the Second Party System. Historians stress the understanding common among participants of reform as being a part of God's plan. As a result, local churches saw their roles in society in purifying the world through the individuals to whom they could bring salvation, and through changes in the law and the creation of institutions. Interest in transforming the world was applied to mainstream political action, as temperance activists, antislavery advocates, and proponents of other variations of reform sought to implement their beliefs into national politics. While religion had previously played an important role on the American political scene, the Second Great Awakening highlighted the important role which individual beliefs would play.

Congregationalists set up missionary societies to evangelize the western territory of the northern tier. Members of these groups acted as apostles for the faith and also as educators and exponents of northeastern urban culture. Publication and education societies promoted Christian education; most notable among them was the American Bible Society, founded in 1816. Social activism influenced abolition groups and supporters of the temperance movement. They began efforts to reform prisons and care for the handicapped and mentally ill. They believed in the perfectibility of people and were highly moralistic in their endeavors. The Second Great Awakening served as an "organizing process" that created "a religious and educational infrastructure" across the western frontier that encompassed social networks, a religious journalism that provided mass communication, and church-related colleges (www.ushistory.org/us/22c.asp).

The Third Great Awakening 1857-1859

Dwight L. Moody, is a well-known leader of the Third Great Awakening. This was a period of religious activism in American history from the late 1850's which affected pietistic Protestant denominations and had a strong sense of social activism. It gathered strength from the postmillennial theology that the Second Coming of Christ would come after mankind had reformed the entire earth. A major component was the Social Gospel Movement, which applied Christianity to social issues and gained its force from the Awakening, as did the worldwide missionary movement. In this time new groupings emerged, such as the Holiness movement and Nazarene movements, and Christian Science (https://www. christianhistoryinstitute.org/magazine/article/wake-of-the-third-great-awakening/).

Again during this time, the Protestant mainline churches were growing rapidly in numbers, wealth and educational levels, throwing off their frontier beginnings and become centered in towns and cities. Intellectuals and writers such as Josiah Strong advocated a muscular Christianity with systematic outreach to the unchurched in America and around the globe.

Others built colleges and universities to train the next generation. Each denomination supported active missionary societies and made the role of missionary one of high prestige. The great majority of pietistic mainline Protestants (in the North) supported the Republican Party and urged it to endorse prohibition and social reforms.

The awakening (1858) was interrupted by the American Civil War while at the same time in the South the Civil War actually stimulated revivals, especially in General Robert E. Lee's army. After the war, Dwight L. Moody made revivalism the centerpiece of his activities in Chicago by founding the Moody Bible Institute.

The hymns of Ira Sankey were especially influential across the nation as "dry's" crusaded in the name of religion for the prohibition of alcohol. The Woman's Christian Temperance Union mobilized Protestant women for social crusades against liquor, pornography, and prostitution, and sparked the demand for woman suffrage (https://www.christianhistoryinstitute.org/magazine/article/wake-of-the-third-great-awakening/).

The Gilded Age plutocracy came under sharp attack from the Social Gospel preachers and with reformers in the Progressive Era. Historian Robert Fogel identifies numerous reforms, especially the battles involving child labor, compulsory elementary education and the protection of women from exploitation in factories (www. regentsprep.org › Regents Prep › U.S. History › Reform).

All the major denominations sponsored growing missionary activities inside the United States and around the world. Colleges associated with churches rapidly expanded in number, size and quality of curriculum. The promotion of "muscular Christianity" became popular among young men on campus and in urban YMCA's, as well as such denominational youth groups such as the Epworth League for Methodists and the Walther League for Lutherans.

Azuza Street Revival

Nearly fifty years after the Third Great Awakening, just as the repetitive cycle predicted, the Church experienced The Azuza Street Revival. It lasted from 1906-1909. William Seymore was a key leader in this movement and as The Apostolic Faith and many secular reports advertised the events of the Azusa Street Revival internationally, thousands of individuals visited the Mission in order to witness it firsthand. At the same time, thousands of people were leaving Azusa Street with the intentions of evangelizing abroad (http://enrichmentjournal.ag.org/199904/026_azusa.cfm).

Reverend K. E. M. Spooner visited the revival in 1909 and became one of the Pentecostal Holiness Church's most effective missionaries in Africa, working among the Tswana people of Botswana. A. G. Garr and his wife were sent from Azusa Street as missionaries to Calcutta, India, where they managed to start a small revival. Speaking in tongues in India did not enable them to speak the native language, Bengali. Garr significantly contributed to early Pentecostalism through his later work in redefining the "biblical evidence" doctrine and changing the doctrine from a belief that speaking in tongues was explicitly for evangelism to a belief that speaking in tongues was a gift for "spiritual empowerment" (http://askthedreamer.com/2012/12/24/legacy-of-azusa-street-a-revival-1906-1915/).

Other visitors left the revival to become missionaries in remote areas all over the world. So many missionaries went out from Azusa (some thirty-eight left in October 1906) that within two years the movement had spread to over fifty nations, including Britain, Scandinavia, Germany, Holland, Egypt, Syria, Palestine, South Africa, Hong Kong, China, Ceylon, and India. Christian leaders visited from all over the world (http://enrichmentjournal. ag.org/200602/200602_164_allpoints.cfm).

Charismatic Movement 1960-1970

The term *Charismatic Movement* is used in varying ways to describe the 20th-century developments in various Christian denominations. It is an ongoing international, cross-denominational/non-denominational Christian movement in which individual, historically mainstream congregations adopt beliefs and practices similar to Pentecostals.

Foundational to the movement is the belief that Christians may be "filled with" or "baptized in" the Holy Spirit as a second experience subsequent to salvation and that it will be evidenced by manifestations of the Holy Spirit. Among Protestants, the movement began around 1960. Among Roman Catholics, it originated around 1967(https://en.wikipedia.org/wiki/Charistmatic_Move).

2008- Present

I believe that the famous leaders of the present awakening are yet to be seen although many have shaped the last two decades. A recent article in Charisma Magazine lists 40 individuals whom they believe have "Radically Changed Our World." One is my father, Dr. Bill Hamon (http://www.charismamag.com/anniversary/40-who-radically-changed-our-world).

While we have seen a great influence, we are still in a time of awakening and there is much yet to be known. One thing we do know is that the United States seems due for a new awakening event. Of course, the people involved have a choice. Will America awaken to God's purpose and make its contribution to the Third Reformation? Again, this is yet to be seen but in the interim we need to pray for our nation!

Awakening Word Study

The term Awakening, as used in the historic sense, is alluded to metaphorically in scripture. In the New Testament, there are several Greek words that can be translated "awaken." The two most common words are:

- *egrio* which is also translated "arise" or "stand up"
- *gregoreo* which is also translated "watch."

These words can be literal, such as when the disciples woke Jesus up in the boat, (Matthew 8:27) or when Jesus woke the disciples on the mountain, (Luke 9:32) or when the angel woke Peter in the prison (Acts 12:7). They can also be figurative to mean becoming aware morally or alert spiritually (Romans 13:11, 1 Corinthians 15:34, and Ephesians 5:14). Further, since sleep is used as a euphemism for death, "awakening" often means to come alive again (John 11:11 and 1 Thessalonians 5:10).

The Old Testament words for "awaken" have a similar range of meaning. The Hebrew words *oor* and *yawkets* simply mean to wake up. There are variations like *koots* which means to wake up abruptly. These words are used literally in stories or figuratively in Psalms, Proverbs, Song of Solomon and many passages in the books of the prophets.

The Hebrew word closest to our historic understanding of awakening is "*shaqad*," It is used in the Psalms: "*Unless the LORD guards the city, the watchman stays awake in vain*" (Psalm 127:1). "*Shaqad*" means to be alert, i.e. sleepless; hence, to be on the lookout whether for good or ill: to hasten, remain, wake, watch (Strong's).

We also find this prophetic sense of awakening in Jeremiah, especially the first chapter, which is the clearest and most powerful prophetic call in scripture.

Then the word of the Lord came to me, saying:
⁵ "Before I formed you in the womb I knew you;
Before you were born I sanctified you;
I ordained you a prophet to the nations."
⁶ Then said I: "Ah, Lord God!
Behold, I cannot speak, for I am a youth."
⁷ But the Lord said to me:
"Do not say, 'I am a youth,'
For you shall go to all to whom I send you,
And whatever I command you, you shall speak.
⁸ Do not be afraid of their faces,
For I am with you to deliver you," says the Lord.
⁹ Then the Lord put forth His hand and touched my mouth, and the Lord said to me:
"Behold, I have put My words in your mouth.
¹⁰ See, I have this day set you over the nations and

> *over the kingdoms,*
> *To root out and to pull down,*
> *To destroy and to throw down,*
> *To build and to plant."*

Jeremiah 1:5-10

Typically, we stop at verse 10 but the call of Jeremiah continues through the rest of chapter 1. In the course of studying the scriptures for awakening, I was particularly drawn to verses 11-12.:

> *Moreover the word of the LORD came to me, saying,*
> *"Jeremiah, what do you see?" And I said, "I see a*
> *branch of an almond tree." Then the LORD said to*
> *me, "You have seen well, for I am ready to perform*
> *My word."*

Jeremiah 1:11-12

Notice in verse 12 the Lord says to Jeremiah *"I am ready to perform My word."* The word "ready" in this verse is the Hebrew word *shaqad*. So this phrase could also be translated: *"I [watch, perform, awaken] to perform My word."*

Since Jeremiah's call is to be over the kingdoms, and his message is primarily to the nation of Israel to awaken to follow God's ways, this verse seems significant to our understanding of awakening especially as it applies to nations and the kingdom.

If verse 12 is significant to awakening to fulfill God's word, then what is the meaning of verse 11? Why does God show Jeremiah *"a branch of an almond tree"*? It turns out that the Hebrew word for almond is *shaqed*, which has a root meaning of the Hebrew word for awakening, or *shaqad*. In Hebrew, the almond tree is literally: *the awakening one.* Here is more detail from The New Unger's

Bible Dictionary:

> Almond, Hebrew *shaqed*, "the awakening one". Its flowers appear as early as February, or even January before the coming of the leaves, so that the appearance of a tree in full bloom is striking. Although the blossoms are tinged with pink, the general effect is white. The fruit is eaten in two stages, the first the tender, acidulous, unripe, crisp pod, and then the seed, which is what we call almonds, so familiar everywhere. This tree is referred to by Jacob in Genesis 43:11, when he tells his sons to take into Egypt, "some of the best products of the land . . . and almonds."

The almond tree signifies awakening, especially the awakening of spring, or a new season of life. So when God shows Jeremiah an almond branch, it makes sense that God's next words are, *"I am awakening to perform My word."* The almond tree would be a clear symbol to Jeremiah that God is declaring a season of significant change.

And so He is…today.

Almond Joy

After discovering the almond tree in Jeremiah, I branched out looking for more "almond" stories and found Korah's rebellion against Moses and Aaron in Numbers 16. For those who unfamiliar with the story, here is a quick recap.

In a daring challenge, Korah leads the people of Israel in a rebellion against the leadership of Aaron, culminating in a standoff on the desert floor. At the height of their insurrection, both sides stand apart from one another—Aaron's people on one side; Korah's people on the other—and the earth splits open and swallows alive all the followers of Korah.

Clearly, God demonstrates His view of the situation with extreme prejudice. However, the unfazed children of Israel wake up the next morning murmuring against Moses and Aaron saying: *"You have killed the people of the LORD."* That's when God's wrath really shows up. A plague starts in camp and over 14,000 people are killed before Aaron, standing between the dead and the living, holds up an incense censer and stops the plague.

With the matter finally settled, God in His mercy establishes a new order for how the people of Israel relate to Him, placing Aaron and hid descendants firmly in front.

> *And the LORD spoke to Moses, saying: "Speak to the children of Israel, and get from them a rod from each father's house...twelve rods. Write each man's name on his rod. And you shall write Aaron's name on the rod of Levi. ... Then you shall place them in the tabernacle of meeting before the Testimony, where I meet with you. And it shall be that the rod of the man whom I choose will blossom... Now it came to pass on the next day that Moses went into the tabernacle of witness, and behold, the rod of Aaron, of the house of Levi, had sprouted and put forth buds, had produced blossoms and yielded ripe almonds.*

> Numbers 17: 1-13

Aaron's rod blooms just as the Lord said, but notice *how* it blooms. It sprouts and puts forth buds, producing blossoms and yielding ripe *almonds*. The almond tree is the "awakening one." It signifies a new season.

The effect of this miracle is immediate and profound.

> *Then the LORD said to Aaron: "You and your sons and your father's house with you shall bear the iniquity related to the sanctuary, and you and your sons with you shall bear the iniquity associated with your priesthood. ...Behold, I Myself have taken your brethren the Levites from among the children of Israel; they are a gift to you, given by the LORD, to do the work of the tabernacle of meeting. Therefore you and your sons with you shall attend to your priesthood for everything at the altar and behind the veil; and you shall serve. I give your priesthood to you as a gift for service, but the outsider who comes near shall be put to death." And the LORD spoke to Aaron: "Here, I Myself have also given you charge of My heave offerings, all the holy gifts of the children of Israel; I have given them as a portion to you and your sons, as an ordinance forever."*
>
> Numbers 18:1-32

Everything has now changed between the people and God. The awakening, heralded by the appearing of the almond tree, has transformed the relationship. The children of Israel now relate to God through the priesthood and the Levites, especially Aaron. This arrangement will remain until Jesus brings a new awakening—the new covenant.

Enlightenment

The Israelites should not have been surprised to see almond

blossoms chosen for Aaron's rod. God had already chosen almond blossoms to display in the tabernacle when He gave the design for the golden lampstand. From The New Unger's Bible Dictionary:

> The golden lampstand (Hebrew *menora*) stood on the left side of the Holy Place, directly opposite the table of showbread (Exodus 40:24). Its construction is minutely described (Exodus 25:31-40; Exodus 37:17-24). The material of which it was made was pure gold. The central shaft and the six branches terminated in sockets into which the seven lamps were placed. The ornamentation of the lampstand consisted of a "cup" (Hebrew *gabîa'*), which was almond-shaped (i.e., the nut), tapering from a head. Above this was the "bulb" (Hebrew *kaptôr*), like the capital of a column, under the intersection of the branches (Exodus 25:35). Surmounting all was the "flower" (Hebrew *perah*, literally "blossom"), like a bud just ready to burst into bloom. Cups shaped like almond blossoms with the oblong oval shape sharpened at one end and rounded at the other was the pattern selected for the bowls of the golden lampstand.

It is noteworthy that all natural light was shut out from the holy place of the Tabernacle; the golden lampstand was the only source of light. It came in the form of almond branches with blossoms signifying God's light awakening us to His purpose and worship.

Light was an important element throughout the time of exodus:

> They did not see one another; nor did anyone rise from his place for three days. But all the children of

Israel had light in their dwellings.

Exodus 10:23

And the LORD went before them by day in a pillar of cloud to lead the way, and by night in a pillar of fire to give them light, so as to go by day and night.

Exodus 13:21,

So it came between the camp of the Egyptians and the camp of Israel. Thus it was a cloud and darkness to the one, and it gave light by night to the other, so that the one did not come near the other all that night.

Exodus 14:20

God gives more specific instructions regarding the lampstand than any other piece of temple furniture. Of course, these instructions are to Aaron and his decedents as priests—the keepers of the tabernacle.

You shall make seven lamps for it, and they shall arrange its lamps so that they give light in front of it.

Exodus 25:37

Speak to Aaron, and say to him, "When you arrange the lamps, the seven lamps shall give light in front of the lampstand."

Numbers 8:2

A significant portion of the offerings brought to the tabernacle are for the lampstand:

And you shall command the children of Israel that they bring you pure oil of pressed olives for the light, to cause the lamp to burn continually.

Exodus 27:20,

Oil for the light, and spices for the anointing oil and for the sweet incense;

Exodus 25:6,

You shall bring in the table and arrange the things that are to be set in order on it; and you shall bring in the lampstand and light its lamps.

Exodus 40:4,

Command the children of Israel that they bring to you pure oil of pressed olives for the light, to make the lamps burn continually. Outside the veil of the Testimony, in the tabernacle of meeting, Aaron shall be in charge of it from evening until morning before the LORD continually; it shall be a statute forever in your generations.

Leviticus 24:2-3,

The appointed duty of Eleazar the son of Aaron the priest is the oil for the light, the sweet incense, the daily grain offering, the anointing oil, the oversight of all the tabernacle, of all that is in it, with the sanctuary and its furnishings."

Numbers 4:16

God is Light

It should be no surprise that God is focused on the lampstand of the tabernacle. Throughout the Bible, God is identified with light. Look at the first thing He does in Genesis.

Then God said, "Let there be light" and there was light.

Genesis 1:3

God is often described as light or the light-provider.

For You will light my lamp; The LORD my God will enlighten my darkness.

Psalm 18:28

This is the message which we have heard from Him and declare to you, that God is light and in Him is no darkness at all.

1 John 1:5

Whose minds the god of this age has blinded, who do not believe, lest the light of the gospel of the glory of Christ, who is the image of God, should shine on them. For we do not preach ourselves, but Christ Jesus the Lord, and ourselves your bondservants for Jesus' sake. For it is the God who commanded light to shine out of darkness, who has shone in our hearts to give the light of the knowledge of the glory of God in the face of Jesus Christ.

2 Corinthians 4:4-6

The New Testament Lampstands

The New Covenant reveals that God does not dwell in a temple. Rather, *we* are the church—the temple of the living God.

And what agreement has the temple of God with idols? For you are the temple of the living God. As

God has said:

"I will dwell in them and walk among them. I will be their God, and they shall be My people."

2 Corinthians 6:16

Yet the meaning of the Old Testament temple furniture and practices still has significance today, and none more than the golden lampstand. In Revelation, the churches are called golden lampstands:

> *[12] Then I turned to see the voice that spoke with me. And having turned I saw seven golden lampstands,[13] and in the midst of the seven lampstands One like the Son of Man, clothed with a garment down to the feet and girded about the chest with a golden band.*

Revelation 1:12-13

The mystery of the seven stars which you saw in My right hand, and the seven golden lampstands: The seven stars are the angels of the seven churches, and the seven lampstands which you saw are the seven churches.

Revelation 1:20

Each church is depicted as a golden lampstand, and Jesus is the high priest who comes to put light into the almond blossoms of each lampstand. The entire purpose of a lampstand is to hold and show the light. It would be ridiculous to have a lampstand and not use it to bring light to a dark situation.

> *No one, when he has lit a lamp, covers it with a vessel or puts it under a bed, but sets it on a lampstand, that those who enter may see the light.*

Luke 8:16-17

No one, when he has lit a lamp, puts it in a secret place or under a basket, but on a lampstand, that those who come in may see the light. The lamp of the body is the eye. Therefore, when your eye is good, your whole body also is full of light. But when your eye is bad, your body also is full of darkness. Therefore take heed that the light which is in you is not darkness. If then your whole body is full of light, having no part dark, the whole body will be full of light, as when the bright shining of a lamp gives you light.

Luke 11:33-36

Following the pattern of priest and temple, in the New Covenant, Jesus is our high priest who brings us the light:

Then Jesus spoke to them again, saying, "I am the light of the world. He who follows Me shall not walk in darkness, but have the light of life."

John 8:12,

While I am in the world, I am the light of the world."

John 9:5

Notice the curious disclaimer Jesus issues to His identification as *"light of the world."* He says: *"as long as I am in the world."* Of course, we know that Jesus is no longer *"in the world."* Rather, He is *"seated at the right hand of the Father"* (Luke 22:69). So does this mean there is no more light in the world? Absolutely not. WE ARE THE LIGHT!

You are the salt of the earth; but if the salt loses its flavor, how shall it be seasoned? It is then good for nothing but to be thrown out and trampled underfoot by men. You are the light of the world. A city that is set on a hill cannot be hidden. Nor do they light a lamp and put it under a basket, but on a lampstand, and it gives light to all who are in the house. Let your light so shine before men, that they may see your good works and glorify your Father in heaven.

Matthew 5:13-16

This scripture ties the light of God directly to good works. It parallels our previous discussion on natural and spiritual perspectives. Most Christians sincerely want to glorify God, but they choose spiritual means to do it: prayer, praise, meditating on His word. This scripture redirects us. Do you want to glorify the Father in heaven? Do good works through the light of the Lord. Use your light to effect change.

We are now the Body of Christ and the Temple of God. Therefore, we are the light of the world.

Now you are the body of Christ, and members individually.

1 Corinthians 12:27

Light is Awakening

Light has a natural awakening quality. Our bodies have built-in circadian rhythms that respond to light. The easiest way to wake a sleeper is to turn on the light. Of course, it's also the easiest way to anger them. (Some people just love darkness, I guess.) Yet, our spirits also respond to light—God's light.

The church is the lampstand. We are the light! Light up your world! Shine with the light of life and wake others to the life of God.

But all things that are exposed are made manifest by the light, for whatever makes manifest is light. Therefore He says: "Awake, you who sleep, Arise from the dead, And Christ will give you light."

Ephesians 5:13-14

Awake to the light Christ has given us. Shine in the darkness wherever you find it. Draw people out of darkness. Awaken the kings of this world to the light.

Arise [awake], shine; for your light has come! And the glory of the LORD is risen upon you. For behold, the darkness shall cover the earth, and deep darkness the people; but the LORD will arise over you, and His glory will be seen upon you. The Gentiles shall come to your light, and kings to the brightness of your rising.

Isaiah 60:1-3

We are the light that wakes the world...and once awake, that transforms it.

9

Kingdom Transformation

The Third Reformation is upon us. The church is growing in power and effectiveness, discovering the importance of hearing God's voice to establish His Kingdom. She is called to be the light of our world to influence culture. As we read in Revelation:

> *Then the seventh angel sounded: And there were loud voices in heaven, saying, "The kingdoms of this world have become the kingdoms of our Lord and of His Christ, and He shall reign forever and ever!"*

Revelation 11:15

Yes, the Third Reformation builds God's Kingdom on earth. So what will this reformation look like? How will it transform lives, communities, cultures, and nations? What can we expect in the coming years? And what of our individual roles?

To understand the future, we must look carefully at the past.

Taken with a bit of scholastic zeal, the concluding stories of the Old Testament are a wonderful illustration of Kingdom reformation. Certainly, every move of God brings its own dynamics. However, study of past moves of God can show us what to expect for the future. Indeed, if we can see the correlations between the Old Testament post-exile stories and the first two reformations, then it seems reasonable to expect the correlation to continue in the Third Reformation.

Combing through the Old Testament, we find correlations as follows.

Reformation	Old Testament	New Testament
First Reformation	Zerubbabel rebuilds the temple	Jesus establishes the church
Second Reformation	Ezra builds the people in God's word	Martin Luther opens God's word to the people
Third Reformation	Nehemiah leads the people to rebuild the walls of Jerusalem	God leads the people to rebuild their cultures as God's Kingdom.

Now, in studying the Old Testament's picture of Kingdom restoration and transformation, we must first realize that the venerable O.T. is not strictly organized chronologically. Because of this, we can have a hard time following a story line while correlating the prophetic voices and historical context. The table below will help us understand the concluding stories of the Old Testament as historical narratives and identify the primary prophetic voices corresponding to these narratives:

O.T. Book	Time Span	Prophet
2 Chronicles	Solomon till the fall of Jerusalem	Jeremiah
Daniel	The captivity in Babylon	Ezekiel
Ezra 1-6	Zerubbabel leads return to Jerusalem	Haggai, Zechariah
Esther	Story of Jews still in Babylon	
Ezra 7-10	Ezra leads a return to Jerusalem	
Nehemiah	Nehemiah leads return to Jerusalem	Malachi

OK, with our road map securely in hand (or our GPS's programmed), let's explore the historical record of these great moves of God.

I. First Reformation Correlation

The Decline and Fall of the Kingdom.

The reign of David's son Solomon in 2 Chronicles marks the beginning of the end for the present Kingdom of Israel. Even though David expanded the kingdom, it is as large and powerful as it will ever be. Solomon inherits a prosperous kingdom that is completely at peace and focuses his energy on building a magnificent temple for God. Solomon, however, does a poor job of building for succession. After Solomon's death, there is a civil war and the kingdom is divided.

Ten of the tribes make up the Northern Kingdom, called Israel. Their kings are not the descendants of David. (See 2 Kings.) The tribes of Judah and Benjamin made up the Southern Kingdom, called Judah. (See 2 Chronicles.) Jerusalem is in Judah and the kings of Judah are the descendants of David. Judah's fortunes fluctuate wildly with each successive king. If a king follows God, the kingdom prospers, but if the king is evil, the kingdom suffers.

There are many prophets in the land: Elijah and Elisha followed by Isaiah then Jeremiah, plus most of the minor prophets: Obadiah, Joel, Micah, Hosea, Jonah, Amos, Nahum, Zephaniah, and Habakkuk.

One of the last truly Godly kings of Judah is Josiah (2 Chronicles 34-35). It is during Josiah's reign that Jeremiah receives his call to prophetic ministry. Unfortunately, Josiah is killed in a battle and the successive kings of Judah are all ungodly. This is when Jeremiah's ministry becomes most active but the people of Judah do not listen to the word of the Lord and are defeated by the Babylonians. The Babylonians allow the king of Judah to remain in power but under Babylonian control. Also, young hostages are taken from the noble families to be raised in Babylon, most notably Daniel.

Following a secession of evil rulers, Zedekiah king of Judah defies God, rejects the prophet Jeremiah, and rebels under Babylonian rule. He might have gotten away with the first two... for a while, but the third action brings swift retribution. King Nebuchadnezzar takes a dim view of the insurrection and returns to destroy Jerusalem (including Solomon's temple), enslaves the survivors and carries them back to Babylon, thus terminating the rebellion with extreme prejudice.

The Kingdom in Exile

All is not lost, however. The fall of Jerusalem as presented in 2 Chronicles invokes a prophecy by Jeremiah and its fulfillment. At this time, Ezekiel begins his prophetic ministry to the Jews in exile. Meanwhile, the story of the Jews in Babylon is carried by Daniel.

Daniel has an amazing career in Babylon. First, he becomes an important advisor to King Nebuchadnezzar. Then he survives a difficult succession from King Nebuchadnezzar to King Belshazzar. Finally, he makes the transition to the court of Cyrus the Great.

During the reign of Darius, Daniel remembers Jeremiah's prophecy that the Jews would return from exile after seventy years, and he sets about to make it happen.

> *In the first year of Darius the son of Ahasuerus, of the lineage of the Medes, who was made king over the realm of the Chaldeans - in the first year of his reign*

I, Daniel, understood by the books the number of the years specified by the word of the LORD through Jeremiah the prophet, that He would accomplish seventy years in the desolations of Jerusalem. Then I set my face toward the Lord God to make request by prayer and supplications, with fasting, sackcloth, and ashes.

Daniel 9:1-3

Now, therefore, our God, hear the prayer of Your servant, and his supplications, and for the Lord's sake cause Your face to shine on Your sanctuary, which is desolate. O my God, incline Your ear and hear; open Your eyes and see our desolations, and the city which is called by Your name; for we do not present our supplications before You because of our righteous deeds, but because of Your great mercies. O Lord, hear! O Lord, forgive! O Lord, listen and act! Do not delay for Your own sake, my God, for Your city and Your people are called by Your name.

Daniel 9:17-19

Daniel begins to pray for the fulfillment of the prophecy. This is one of the great intercessory prayers in scripture. There are many wonderful elements to this prayer but the one of interest for this teaching is Daniel's recurring emphasis of praying not just for the people or the nation but for the city of Jerusalem:

We will see this emphasis on Jerusalem again in Nehemiah.

The Return of the King

Now Ezra takes up the story. The Jews have been in Babylon

for 70 years and Cyrus the Great is king. Quite unexpectedly, Cyrus proclaims that God commanded him to build the temple in Jerusalem.

> Now in the first year of Cyrus king of Persia, that the word of the LORD by the mouth of Jeremiah might be fulfilled, the LORD stirred up the spirit of Cyrus king of Persia, so that he made a proclamation throughout all his kingdom, and also put it in writing, saying,
>
> Thus says Cyrus king of Persia:
>
> "All the kingdoms of the earth the LORD God of heaven has given me. And He has commanded me to build Him a house at Jerusalem which is in Judah. Who is among you of all His people? May his God be with him, and let him go up to Jerusalem which is in Judah, and build the house of the LORD God of Israel (He is God), which is in Jerusalem. And whoever is left in any place where he dwells, let the men of his place help him with silver and gold, with goods and livestock, besides the freewill offerings for the house of God which is in Jerusalem."
>
> Then the heads of the fathers' houses of Judah and Benjamin, and the priests and the Levites, with all whose spirits God had moved, arose to go up and build the house of the LORD which is in Jerusalem. And all those who were around them encouraged them with articles of silver and gold, with goods and livestock, and with precious things, besides all that was willingly offered. King Cyrus also brought out the articles of the house of the LORD, which Nebuchadnezzar had

taken from Jerusalem and put in the temple of his gods; and Cyrus king of Persia brought them out by the hand of Mithredath the treasurer, and counted them out to Sheshbazzar the prince of Judah.

Ezra 1:1-8

Cyrus responds to the voice of God by recruiting a group of Jewish people to return to Jerusalem and rebuild the temple. Cyrus allows the Jews in Babylon to support the project financially; he also returns all the articles that Nebuchadnezzar had removed. Cyrus puts "Sheshbazzar the Prince of Judah" in charge of the whole project. Sheshbazzar is the Babylonian name for Zerubbabel. He becomes the governor (Haggai 1:14) of the Jews who return from Babylonian exile under Cyrus' permission, c. 537 BC.

This is significant because Zerubbabel, leading the first returning band of exiles, is a grandson of King Jehoiachin. Hence Zerubbabel is the rightful heir to the throne of Judah. Following his lead, 50,000 Jews return to Israel to begin rebuilding of the Temple in 536 BC. (Ezra 3:8-13).

Of course, nobody said it was going to be easy. The local authorities around Jerusalem are against the rebuilding of the temple, so when Cyrus dies they petitioned the new king Cambyses to cancel the project. The rebuilding stops (Ezra 4:24) shortly after the foundation is complete. Fortunately, sixteen years later there was a new king, Darius I. In King Darius's second year, the two prophets, Haggai and Zechariah, begin to prophesy and urge resumption of the building. Zerubbabel, along with Joshua, the high priest, responds (Ezra 5:1-2; Haggai 1:12). The work is reauthorized by Darius and is completed in the spring of 515 BC.

Besides leading the rebuilding, Zerubbabel also restores

both the priests and Levites to the proper function in the temple (Ezra 6:18).

The First Reformation Foreshadowed

Parallels between Zerubbabel and Jesus abound. Zerubbabel was the heir of the throne of David just as Jesus was (and is) the heir of the throne of David.

> *He will be great, and will be called the Son of the Highest; and the Lord God will give Him the throne of His father David. Jesus came to lead captives to freedom.*
>
> Luke 1:32
>
> *Therefore He says: "When He ascended on high, He led captivity captive, And gave gifts to men."*
>
> Ephesians 4:8

Zerubbabel led 50,000 exiles out of Babylon back to Jerusalem. He came with the authority of the God of heaven to rebuild the temple. In like manner, Jesus came to build the temple of God in all believers and led captivity captive.

> *"Do you not know that you are the temple of God and that the Spirit of God dwells in you?"*
>
> 1 Corinthians 3:16
>
> *"And I also say to you that you are Peter, and on this rock I will build My church, and the gates of Hades shall not prevail against it.*
>
> Matthew 16:18

Jesus answered and said to them, "Destroy this temple, and in three days I will raise it up."

John 2:19

"When He ascended on high, He led captivity captive, and gave gifts to men."

Ephesians 4:8

Notice how God begins His kingdom reformation by establishing His presence through worship. The temple is a place to worship God. It is a place for God to inhabit; God inhabits the praises of His people. The first requirement for reformation, therefore, is a proper relationship with the Lord. And to do that, *the temple must be set in order.* We will see this pattern repeatedly throughout the concluding Old Testament stories. Let's look at a few and discover what they reveal.

II. Second Reformation Correlation

The Return of the Priest

Things are looking up for the restoration of Jewish culture. The temple is rebuilt and the priests and Levites are restored for proper worship. Then, at the end of Ezra 6, there is a 57-year gap before the beginning of Ezra 7. This gap contains the story of Esther. King Xerxes (called Ahasuerus in Hebrew) makes Esther his queen in 479 BC. This is a difficult time of accusations against the people in Israel. We know from Esther's story that she, along with her uncle Mordecai, becomes influential in Babylon and willingly advocates for the welfare of God's people. It is fascinating to speculate on the influence Esther and Mordecai may have had to facilitate the projects in Jerusalem.

Our story continues in Ezra 7, with the second return of the Jews led by Ezra. Ezra is an unusual person in Babylon. First, we know that he is the descendant of Aaron the chief priest

Now after these things, in the reign of Artaxerxes king of Persia, Ezra the son … of Aaron the chief priest.

Ezra 7:5

Ezra lives in Babylon but he is also a recognized scholar and teacher of the law of God.

this Ezra came up from Babylon; and he was a skilled scribe in the Law of Moses, which the Lord God of Israel had given. The king granted him all his request, according to the hand of the Lord his God upon him.

Ezra 7:6

Once again, the Babylonian king, this time Artaxerxes, gives the Jews led by Ezra permission to return to Jerusalem. The king also provides funds, materials, support personnel, and a tax exemption for the project.

Perhaps the most extraordinary feature about Ezra is his "life purpose. "

For Ezra had prepared his heart to seek the Law of the LORD, and to do it, and to teach statutes and ordinances in Israel.

Ezra 7:10

Ezra's entire focus is to teach God's word to God's people. Ezra needs temple workers to accomplish this mission but when he organizes his group, the Levites are missing

Now I gathered them by the river that flows to Ahava,

and we camped there three days. And I looked among the people and the priests, and found none of the sons of Levi there.

Ezra 8:15

So Ezra recruits them heavily from the Levite families in Babylon and they respond.

Then, by the good hand of our God upon us, they brought us a man of understanding, of the sons of Mahli the son of Levi, the son of Israel, namely Sherebiah, with his sons and brothers, eighteen men.

Ezra 8:18

The result is that some of the children of Israel, along with the priests, the Levites, the singers, the gatekeepers, and the Nethinim come up to Jerusalem in the seventh year of King Artaxerxes.

When Ezra arrives in Jerusalem, he first makes sure that the temple is fully equipped, funded, and staffed. Next, he begins his mission to teach the people God's ways. He quickly finds that the people are not properly following God's way, particularly regarding intermarriage that leads to idolatry. Ezra first intercedes for the people (Ezra 9:6- 15). Then he brings reforms to the leaders in the temple.

Then Ezra arose, and made the leaders of the priests, the Levites, and all Israel swear an oath that they would do according to this word. So they swore an oath.

Ezra 10:5

Next, he gathers the people to teach them God's law and guides them to reform their practices.

So all the men of Judah and Benjamin gathered at Jerusalem within three days. …Then Ezra the priest stood up and said to them, "You have transgressed and have taken pagan wives, adding to the guilt of Israel."

Ezra 10:9-10

Finally, Ezra sets up a system to help every individual household come into alignment with God's Word

Then the descendants of the captivity did so. And Ezra the priest, with certain heads of the fathers' households, were set apart by the fathers' households, each of them by name; and they sat down on the first day of the tenth month to examine the matter.

Ezra 10:16

The Second Reformation Foreshadowed

Just as Zerubbabel parallels Jesus and the First Reformation, so we find similar parallels with Ezra and Martin Luther of the Second Reformation. Ezra was a priest, scholar, and teacher. Martin Luther was also a priest, scholar, and teacher, as were nearly all the leaders of the Second Reformation. Ezra reformed the practices of the temple leadership. Martin Luther eventually reformed the practices of the church leadership. Ezra's mission was teaching the people how to understand God's Word so they can relate to Him properly. Martin Luther's main issue was for every believer to have a proper understanding of the Word of God so he or she can have a personal righteous relationship with God.

The people must know God, His statutes and His ways.

III. Third Reformation Correlation

The Return of the Saints

The story of the restoration of the Kingdom should end with Ezra, right? At least that is what my theology and training leads me to expect. After all, the temple has been built and is functioning properly. The people have been taught and are following God's ways. What more do we need? Yet after 12 years of temple worship and priestly ministry, we come to the concluding story of the Old Testament in the book of Nehemiah.

Nehemiah is a man who works for the king of Babylon as his cupbearer. He has a very important position in the court that gives him direct access to the king. Traditionally, part of the cupbearer's duties is literally to protect the king from poisoning. We can also surmise that Nehemiah is wealthy and influential in Babylon. Nehemiah is not descended from kings (like Zerubbabel) or from priests (like Ezra). He is an ordinary man who has become successful in a secular environment. One might say that his cup runneth over.

In chapter 1, Nehemiah gets news from Judah. Nehemiah's brother returns from a business trip and reports: *"The survivors who are left from the captivity in the province are there in great distress and reproach. The wall of Jerusalem is also broken down, and its gates are burned with fire."* (v3)

Nehemiah has a dramatic reaction to this news. *"So it was, when I heard these words, that I sat down and wept, and mourned for many days; I was fasting and praying before the God of heaven."* (v4) Nehemiah then makes an intercessory prayer in verses 5-11.

During my study, I was surprised by Nehemiah's reaction. The temple had been restored for over 70 years and Ezra is still there to teach and lead the people to follow God. Why is Nehemiah so distressed to learn the walls and gates of the city are still broken down? I needed to understand Nehemiah. I had to see what the walls and gates of the city really meant, and why news of their destruction was received with so much trauma.

The Gates of the City

Ancient cities were often more like fortresses than cities, as we understand the term "city" today. The perimeter consisted of a massive stone wall with gates to permit or prevent the entry of people and animals. There were ten gates in Jerusalem that were named in Nehemiah chapter 3; starting at the north and moving counterclockwise: Sheep Gate, Fish Gate, Old Gate, Valley Gate, Refuse Gate, Fountain Gate, Water Gate, Horse Gate, East Gate, and Miphkad Gate.

Other scriptures clearly indicate the importance of the city walls and gates beyond just defensive structures. Old Testament examples include:

> *You shall appoint judges and officers in all your gates, which the Lord your God gives you, according to your tribes, and they shall judge the people with just judgment.*
>
> Deuteronomy 16:18

> *And all the people who were at the gate, and the elders, said, "We are witnesses."*
>
> Ruth 4:11

These stories in the Old Testament refer to "elders in the gates." The elders are in the gates because the gates are where business is done and legal cases are heard. In the New Testament we see:

Enter by the narrow gate; for wide is the gate and broad is the way that leads to destruction, and there are many who go in by it.

Matthew 7:13

Blessed are those who do His commandments that they may have the right to the tree of life, and may enter through the gates into the city.

Revelation 22:14

I will build My church, and the gates of Hades shall not prevail against it.

Matthew 16:18

In the description of the new Jerusalem, a great emphasis is given to the walls and gates of the city.

Also she had a great and high wall with twelve gates, and twelve angels at the gates, and names written on them, which are the names of the twelve tribes of the children of Israel: three gates on the east, three gates on the north, three gates on the south, and three gates on the west. Now the wall of the city had twelve foundations, and on them were the names of the twelve apostles of the Lamb. … The twelve gates were twelve pearls: each individual gate was of one pearl.

Revelation 21:12-14

As we said earlier, gates to the ancient cities were more than defensive structures. They were places of commerce and government. The power and authority of the city operated in the gates. Although we often spiritualize the names of the gates in

Jerusalem, the original names were practical. The "fish gate" was not about saving souls; it was about buying and selling fish. The "water gate" was not about the infilling of the Spirit; it led to the source of water for the city.

The value of city walls as defensive structures diminished in the late 15th century with the introduction of siege cannons powerful enough to turn them to rubble. The use of city walls and gates for commercial and legal transactions became lost by the 18th century with population explosions in cities that accompanied the industrial revolution. Even with these modern changes, however, the old walled city has become the new city center and still maintains its original commercial, legal, and religious significance. You can see this in modern Jerusalem's Old City district and downtown areas of cities like Rome, Paris, and London.

For example: American cities were mostly developed in the late 18th century and were built without walls, but with one notable exception. In 1652, the Dutch established a city called New Amsterdam with a wall near the confluence of the Hudson river and the East river. The wall had a defensive purpose against natives and other colonialist but it also became the center of business and authority in the city. The first church, the first city hall, and the first businesses were all built along the wall. The British took over the city and renamed it New York. The wall was dismantled in 1699 but the street that served the wall remained and retained its importance in the city. Today this street in New York City is called Wall Street and is considered by many as the commercial center of the world.

Now we can better understand why Nehemiah was so distressed when he heard that the walls and gates of Jerusalem were destroyed.

Without walls and gates, the city had no life, no commerce, and no authority. Jesus understood this when He said, *"On this rock I will build My church, and the gates of Hades shall not prevail against it"* (Matthew 16:18).

Now I understood why Nehemiah accepted the call to transform the city by rebuilding its wall and gates. Likewise, the first thing the reformed church must do is engage the gates; they represent the power and authority we must reclaim to go forth and transform our culture.

The Third Reformation Foreshadowed.

As parallels to the Third Reformation, there are many lessons from Nehemiah on how to be successful in cultural transformation. Let us examine a few:

1. Passion For The City

Nehemiah's consuming passion was to see the city restored to its true function as God intended.

> *"Why should my face not be sad, when the city, the place of my fathers' tombs, lies waste, and its gates are burned with fire?" Then the king said to me, "What do you request?" So I prayed to the God of heaven. And I said to the king, "If it pleases the king, and if your servant has found favor in your sight, I ask that you send me to Judah, to the city of my fathers' tombs, that I may rebuild it."*
>
> Nehemiah 2:3-5

2. Partner With Diverse People

Nehemiah was not afraid to recruit all kinds of people to work to rebuild the city. Indeed, his genius was in involving the entire community. In the verses of chapter 3, we see that repairs for each part of the wall were delegated to a different group. In modern terms the list would correspond as follows:

Nehemiah 3:1—priests;

3:2—neighboring communities;

3:3—city residents;

3:8—professionals and tradesmen;

3:9—local government;

3:12—women;

3:17—religious groups and charities;

3:22—other temple workers;

3:23—local residents;

3:32—merchants.

3. No Compromise with the Enemy.

The enemy constantly harassed and attacked Nehemiah and his workers. When direct threats did not work, the enemy tried to deceive him into a vulnerable position:

> Now it happened when Sanballat, Tobiah, Geshem the Arab, and the rest of our enemies heard that I had rebuilt the wall, and that there were no breaks left in it (though at that time I had not hung the doors in the gates), that Sanballat and Geshem sent to me, saying, 'Come, let us meet together among the villages in the plain of Ono.' But they thought to do me harm. So I sent messengers to them, saying, 'I am doing a great work, so that I cannot come down. Why should the work cease while I leave it and go down to you?'"

> Nehemiah 6:1-3

Next, the enemies tried to intimidate Nehemiah by false accusations:

Then Sanballat sent his servant to me as before, the fifth time, with an open letter in his hand. In it was written: It is reported among the nations, and Geshem says, that you and the Jews plan to rebel; therefore, according to these rumors, you are rebuilding the wall, that you may be their king. ⁷ And you have also appointed prophets to proclaim concerning you at Jerusalem, saying, "There is a king in Judah!" Now these matters will be reported to the king. So come, therefore, and let us consult together. Then I sent to him, saying, "No such things as you say are being done, but you invent them in your own heart." For they all were trying to make us afraid, saying, "Their hands will be weakened in the work, and it will not be done." Now therefore, O God, strengthen my hands."

Nehemiah 6:5-9

Finally, they tried a combination of deception and religious manipulation to trick Nehemiah into a compromising situation in:

Afterward I came to the house of Shemaiah the son of Delaiah, the son of Mehetabel, who was a secret informer; and he said, "Let us meet together in the house of God, within the temple, and let us close the doors of the temple, for they are coming to kill you; indeed, at night they will come to kill you." And I said, "Should such a man as I flee? And who is there such as I who would go into the temple to save his life? I will not go in!" Then I perceived that God had not sent him at all, but that he pronounced this prophecy against me because Tobiah and Sanballat had hired him. For this reason he was hired, that I should be afraid and act that way and sin, so that they might have cause for an evil report, that they might reproach me."

Nehemiah 6:10-13

Nehemiah always trusted in what God told him and never compromised with the enemy.

4. Equip the People to Build and Fight

The mission to build the wall was great and the threats against the project were serious. Nehemiah made sure everyone was equipped to build and to fight.

Those who built on the wall, and those who carried burdens, loaded themselves so that with one hand they worked at construction, and with the other held a weapon. Every one of the builders had his sword girded at his side as he built. And the one who sounded the trumpet was beside me. He made sure that everyone could hear the trumpet call to know when to come to the battle.

Notice that Nehemiah gave the people three things:

- tools to work
- weapons to fight
- a trumpet to hear

While the first two items seem common sense, few notice the third—the trumpet. Somehow, hearing gets left off the list of cool stuff needed to build and fight in a hostile environment. But in fact, warrior-builders must first and foremost be able to hear and respond to the call to arms. Peter rocked the garden the day he showed Jesus he was finally hearing God. From that point forward, he was a builder under Jesus: *"on this rock I will build..."* (Matthew 16:18).

5. Never Waver in Supporting the Temple.

We know that Nehemiah was focused on reforming the city by rebuilding the walls and gates, yet he consistently supported the temple, including the priests and Levites. We see him actually requiring the leaders of the city to sign a contract saying, *"We will not neglect the house of our God"* (Nehemiah 10:39).

Nehemiah returned to Babylon (chapter 13) but then the prophet Malachi had to remind the people of their obligation to God. Finally, Nehemiah returned to Jerusalem to reestablish the reformation shocked by what he found, crying out: *"Why is the house of God Neglected?"* (Nehemiah 13:11). They then proceeded to clean house, both figuratively and literally. The final story of the Old Testament in Nehemiah 13 and the final prophecy in Malachi are focused on a proper response to God's temple.

The Third Reformation Summary

Yes, to transform our culture, we must first and foremost support the temple—the assembly for equipping the saints. But we must also get our hands dirty, engaging with people we might not otherwise associate with, expanding our skills in everything from blueprint reading and construction to zoning laws and community activism. We must also learn to deal with the inevitable secular and religious threats to rebuilding the centers of power and government under the influence of the Kingdom of God.

The Third Reformation is the culmination of God's Kingdom building on earth. The people of God need to get a vision for rebuilding the walls and gates to establish righteousness and justice in the culture. We are working like Nehemiah to transform our cultures. Only then will we hear *"Then the seventh angel sounded: And there were loud voices in heaven, saying, "The kingdoms of this world have become the kingdoms of our Lord and of His Christ, and He shall reign forever and ever!"* (Revelation 11:15).

In our final chapter, we will look further into the specifics for this awesome assignment set before us.

10

What Must We Then Do?

Before we can expect the kingdoms of this world to become the Kingdoms of God, we must do the work of Nehemiah and transform our cultures. We must be a light in our world and awaken the kings of the world's kingdoms to the knowledge of the glory of Christ the King. Our authority to transform lives and cultures is predicated on hearing God's Voice.

When God's Voice Brings Transformation

From the beginning of recorded history, the voice of God carried the power to transform. *"Then God said, 'Let there be light'; and there was light"* (Genesis 1:3). Please note that when God said *"Let there be light,"* He was not describing light. He was creating light!

Throughout history, the voice of God changes people. A bumbling apostle heard the voice of God and it transformed him from Simon (a shaking reed) to Peter (a solid rock). (Matthew 16: 17-18.) A murderous zealot heard the voice of God and was transformed from Saul to Paul. A childless nomad heard the voice of God and was transformed from Abram to Abraham.

God is speaking to each of us today about the Third Reformation. It is our responsibility to respond to the transforming word of God. Everyone who hears His voice must respond in their own specific way, specific to their situation, calling, and faith.

There is an ongoing shift in the function of the church. No longer are we satisfied to simply see the lost saved and sanctified while waiting for Christ's return. NO! Now we see our true function—to bring transformation to the world around us. We must establish the Kingdom of God in every culture so that *"The kingdom of the world has become the kingdom of our Lord, and His Christ; and He will reign forever and ever"* (Revelations 11:15).

The Kingdom Message changes how we think, what we do, and how we implement. It changes our focus and thus our goals and objectives toward ministry. It calls us to develop new wineskins ready for the new wine. Everything we have done, everything we are doing, and everything we will do must undergo a rigorous transformation. To stay relevant with the current move of God, new wineskins must stay new.

As we establish a unity of faith and vision, we recognize the diverse calling God has placed on each of us. Even God describes Himself as *one* yet *three* expressions.

> *For there are three that bear witness in heaven: the Father, the Word, and the Holy Spirit; and these three are one."*

> 1 John 5:7

We are one Body. God made us one identity in Him.

> *It has now been revealed by the Spirit to God's holy apostles and prophets. This mystery is that through*

the gospel the Gentiles are heirs together with Israel,
members together of one body, and sharers together
in the promise in Christ Jesus.

Ephesians 3:5-6

These scriptures use the human body as an illustration of the Body of Christ. Modern science tells us the human body is made up of many interdependent networks of tissues and organs with different functions: cardiovascular, respiratory, nervous, skin, musculoskeletal, blood, digestive, endocrine, urinary, and reproductive. Every part must play its part for the whole body to prosper.

The body is a unit, though it is made up of many
parts; and though all its parts are many, they form
one body. So it is with Christ. For we were all baptized
by one Spirit into one body—whether Jews or Greeks,
slave or free - and we were all given the one Spirit to
drink. Now the body is not made up of one part but
of many. If the foot should say, "Because I am not a
hand, I do not belong to the body," it would not for
that reason cease to be part of the body. And if the ear
should say, "Because I am not an eye, I do not belong
to the body," it would not for that reason cease to be
part of the body. If the whole body were an eye, where
would the sense of hearing be? If the whole body were
an ear, where would the sense of smell be? But in fact
God has arranged the parts in the body, every one
of them, just as he wanted them to be. If they were
all one part, where would the body be? As it is, there
are many parts, but one body. The eye cannot say to

the hand, "I don't need you!" And the head cannot say to the feet, "I don't need you!" On the contrary, those parts of the body that seem to be weaker are indispensable, and the parts that we think are less honorable we treat with special honor. And the parts that are unpresentable are treated with special modesty, while our presentable parts need no special treatment. But God has combined the members of the body and has given greater honor to the parts that lacked it, so that there should be no division in the body, but that its parts should have equal concern for each other. If one part suffers, every part suffers with it; if one part is honored, every part rejoices with it. Now you are the body of Christ, and each one of you is a part of it.

1 Corinthians 12:12-30 (NIV)

In the Body of Christ, this diversity is expressed in how local churches serve their communities. Each church must find its own way to exert Kingdom influence in their culture. Just as each believer must recognize the mountain they are called to, each local body must realize its mission to be accomplished. Our common Kingdom vision is expressed uniquely through our diverse gifts and cultural context.

Unity in Diversity

We are diverse yet united. Every part of the body comes from the *same DNA* expressed through the *same base set of stem-cells*, and every part is *controlled by one brain*.

It was he who gave some to be apostles, some to be

prophets, some to be evangelists, and some to be pastors and teachers, to prepare God's people for works of service, so that the body of Christ may be built up until we all reach unity in the faith and in the knowledge of the Son of God and become mature, attaining to the whole measure of the fullness of Christ. Then we will no longer be infants, tossed back and forth by the waves, and blown here and there by every wind of teaching and by the cunning and craftiness of men in their deceitful scheming. Instead, speaking the truth in love, we will in all things grow up into him who is the Head, that is, Christ. From him the whole body, joined and held together by every supporting ligament, grows and builds itself up in love, as each part does its work.

Ephesians 4:11-16,

We must embrace our differences within our unity. Like the human body with its various interconnected networks of organs, we should embrace the strength of diverse function while strictly adhering to our fundamental common identity as given by Jesus.

Jesus replied: "Love the Lord your God with all your heart and with all your soul and with all your mind. This is the first and greatest commandment. And the second is like it: Love your neighbor as yourself. All the Law and the Prophets hang on these two commandments."

Matthew 22:37-40

The love of God is our common identity. Loving our neighbor is our strength in diversity. How you respond to the revelation of Kingdom and Third Reformation determines your role in it. Membership is not admittance into an elitist club. Instead, it is the natural alliance of believers hearing the same thing: the voice of God.

<u>Appendix</u>

I Hear Voices!

Yes, I do. Of course, we all hear voices. Not just the natural voices that surround us—media, friends, family, or neighbors. We also have voices inside ourselves. We hear ourselves think, we have jolts of intuition, we remember voices from our past, we imagine voices in our future, and occasionally we get tongue-lashings from our conscience. Hey, it's noisy in there!

Throughout this book, I refer to the voice of God. This begs the question: among the myriad of voices assaulting our consciousness from within and without, can we really hear the voice of God?

Of course we can.

First of all, experiencing the voice of God is a matter of faith. Believing He will do something is generally a requirement for experiencing it. Further, scripture promises that when we ask a good thing, our Father in heaven will never give us a bad thing. Hearing from God is a good thing.

In my experience, most Christians believe God communicates to them in some way or another. But in the next breath, they put severe restrictions on how, why, and what He communicates. Some groups believe He only communicates through the Scriptures. Others believe He can use inspired preaching or prophetic utterances. Some folks look for signs in the heavens—literal cloud formations. And a few enterprising souls expect serendipitous occurrences as indications from the Almighty: numbers on subway schedules, random license plate sightings, even tunes that "jump out" at them as they flip through channels. While each of these ways is fine, each condition we put on God tends to disqualify us from receiving from Him in the myriad ways that He speaks.

I grew up in a classical Pentecostal environment. Amidst all the good I gleaned from such a raising, I also encountered a form of "hyper-spirituality" in the emotional trappings people applied to hearing from God. Somehow, the voice, the leading, the unction, the direction, the word…couldn't be from God if it wasn't accompanied by screaming, shouting, jumping, and passing out.

For years, I wondered what was wrong with me as I sat silently in my pew, observing it all with detached fascination. Then I realized that, for me, the voice of God is a quiet inspiration that reveals Him within the context of reason and rational choice. God made me as heart, mind, and emotions (at least, I think I have emotions…) and He knows what I need. Some people thrive on the exuberance of supernatural experiences. For my part, God and I think together. I am at peace to "think" toward God and have Him "think" back to me. *"Come now, and let us reason together,' says the Lord…"* (Isaiah 1:18, NKJV). Once I accepted that the God who created me was the God who related to me, the supernatural experience of communicating with God became alive. We are all different and God relates to us as we are, speaking to us in ways that are as diverse as the human experience.

Appendix

Throughout Scripture, we see God continually communicating with people in various ways. We see Him speaking aloud on mountaintops, bellowing from clouds, or sending words via an angel: *"Thus says the Lord: Fear NOT!"* However, those spectacular ways are rare. Usually, the conversation is conversational such as David asking God for guidance and encouragement, or Jesus communicating with His Father about His destiny. In truth, God can speak to anyway He wishes: a dream or vision, a fellow believer or an angel. It can be a still small voice during your prayer time. It can be an illumination of Scripture that you never saw that way before. Whatever way He speaks to you, let Him. He's your Father and He wants to speak. Let Him.

The mistake we often make is imitating Elijah in the cave expecting to find God in the dramatic. We seek God's voice in the fire, or earthquake, or violent wind. Instead, it often comes as a still, small voice. Yet it's perfectly understandable to expect the same voice that initiated the Big Bang to have a little POW! to it—or to at least sound like Morgan Freedman—but such thinking misses the true nature of God's voice. He wants us to seek Him, listening for Him, drawing near to His voice rather than getting knocked over by it.

Fundamentally, God wants to speak to us as any father speaks to his children. Indeed, He is eager and quite able to reach us. And given that we serve an all-powerful God who yearns to communicate with us, I'll give you a moment to figure out where the barrier lies. It is somewhere between us and Him…closer to us, I think. The barrier is our inability to hear Him. This is why the Scripture admonishes us: *"Whoever has ears to hear, let them hear"* (Luke 8:8).

Jesus was in regular communication with the Father, not to receive direction for His every step but for encouragement, inspiration, and guidance from His good Father. The good news is that this is what He wants to be for us also—a good Father who speaks when we need Him. He gives us what we need through the power of His voice.

From Genesis throughout the entire Old Testament, we see God speaking, pleading, even crying out to man. Then Jesus arrives declaring *"My sheep hear my voice"* (John 10:27), and the entire New Testament is filled with God continually speaking to people. You know, I think God likes to talk!

So how do we know what we are hearing is the voice of God? After all, you don't want to listen to every voice outside or inside your head—especially when those voices start quarreling. For Christians, the ultimate arbiter of God's communication is the Bible. All communication that is from God must align with the principles and character of God as described in the Scriptures. No exceptions. Without a clear standard to validate the essential quality of any communication, we are prone to a host of deception. This is why John tells us: *"Dear friends, do not believe every spirit, but test the spirits to see whether they are from God"* (1 John 4:1). God certainly communicates today, but it always lines up with what He has been saying and doing for thousands of years.

Do not let the fear of deception deter you, however. If you're a believer in Jesus Christ, Scripture clearly says you should be able to hear *His* voice. *"My sheep listen to my voice; I know them, and they follow me"* (John 10:27). Please receive this truth and pursue it. Take some time, explore, accept that you might make some mistakes, and admit the Spirit of God into your consciousness in ways that allow Him to communicate clearly. He loves you; let Him in.

Interestingly, scripture detailing Peter's realization that Jesus was the Christ never spells out *how* Peter got that revelation. Did he hear an angel? Did God breath it into him? Did the clouds form the words above him? Did a New York City yellow cab bearing the custom plate "HESLORD" honk its horn just as Peter stepped off a curb? Who knows? Jesus' obvious joy was in the fact that Peter got it at all. If the method of Peter's receiving was important, scripture would tell us. It doesn't. Instead, it gives us two salient points: Peter got it, and it revealed the Lordship of Jesus Christ.

Be like Peter. Communicate with God in a way that works best for you: quiet time, jogging, fasting, feasting, worshiping, reading the Bible, reading War and Peace, talking with friends, climbing a mountain, writing a song, painting a sunset, running a boiler, tossing a toddler into the air, meditating on the wonders of God's love. Just remember to test the spirits. *"Every spirit that acknowledges that Jesus Christ has come in the flesh is from God, 3 but every spirit that does not acknowledge Jesus is not from God"* (1 John 4:2-3).

When we can hear God, we can do His work. Let's build His Kingdom together.

About The Author

Dr. Tim Hamon serves as the CEO of Christian International Ministries Network and president of CI School of Theology. He is an instructor, author and international conference keynote speaker.

He was ordained to the ministry in 1988 and earned a Doctorate of Philosophy in Organizational Leadership from Regent University in 2003. Before that, Tim earned his Bachelor of Science from Southern Methodist University and Master of Science from Arizona State University. Tim subsequently worked a decade in the computer industry as a professional engineer. Thus, he brings a full range of business, education, and ministry experience to his teaching.

Tim and his beautiful wife Karen (of 37 years) reside in Santa Rosa Beach, Florida. They have four children, two married, Ruth to Jason and Sheri to Rich; and two single, Sarah and Tim II. And five grandchildren: Cyrus, Grace, Ian, Ezra, Eli. Every member of his family is a follower of Jesus Christ.

Tim has a passion to see every believer equipped to fulfill his or her ministry call and thereby help the Body of Christ grow toward perfection. He is loved and respected for both his teaching gift and his dry sense of humor.

Citations

I am blessed to live in a time of powerful Bible study software. I have the books on my shelves: Bible translations, Bible dictionaries and handbooks, lexicons, interlinear, commentaries, concordances, systematic theology, historical writings, and many other tools as well as books by contemporary authors. I have to admit that most of these books are gathering dust because they, and many more, are available in the software. For many years I used WordSearch [www.wordsearchbible.com]. For the last few years I have used Logos Bible software [www.logos.com]. Both are excellent tools.

One advantage to software is the ability to use multiple sources simultaneously. That is, I can easily read multiple dictionaries or commentaries or anything else simply by selecting the resource from the virtual library. This allows me to explore topics from various theological schools of thought or other diverse perspectives. The only downside is I find myself often unable to cite a specific work. Rather I want to make statements like "Commentaries generally agree that …" I know that is not very helpful to the reader but I hope you understand. I encourage you to invest in good software tools.

I also make a number of historical references, especially during my discussion of reformation. Again, this is general knowledge drawn from multiple sources: encyclopedias, history texts, web sites, etc. So again, I have not cited specific works.

About Christian International

Christian International's vision is to establish Apostles and Prophets, to equip the Saints to transform the world so that Christ may return.

As the rising tide of global advancement lifts economies, so the church rises with them. Advances in technology, medicine, education, and civil rights are affecting not only the secular community, but the Christian community as well. Our ability to impact the cultures of the world are being enhanced by advancements within those world cultures.

The call to transform the world means that we, His Church, are called to equip Saints to go forth in unity of purpose and vision to impact and transform our communities, cities, and nations. At Christian International (C.I.), we recognize that our core strength is, and always will be, the prophetic. Further, we will continue to do things with great strength: training leaders and activating the prophetic, raising up churches and ministries around the world, and equipping the local church pastor. This means that we focus on our core strengths in each area of the ministry so that we are more able to build new areas. This message changes us; it changes me.

Therefore, our first response is unity and focus: CI has one Lord, one Faith, one Vision. Our second response: CI has one vision but many expressions.

Of course, I must also respond to God's voice in my own life. My job is the Chief Executive Officer at Christian International Ministries Network (known as Christian International or CI). We have heard the Voice of God and so we are beginning to respond and to be transformed.

The original vision of CI was: "to establish Apostles and Prophets to equip the Saints for the coming of the Lord." Using this vision, CI has developed training materials that are used around the globe. We have trained and activated thousands of individuals to operate and function in the prophetic, including intercession, worship, the arts, and business. We have been used to educate thousands of degree-seeking students. We have been instrumental in establishing ministries worldwide, and we have a significant presence in the realm of marketplace ministry.

CI's keynote scripture is "apostles and prophets ... equip the saints" (Ephesians 4:11). However, as we heard the revelation of the Kingdom and Seven Mountains, we realized that our vision was incomplete. Therefore, the Christian International vision has been expanded to include "transform the world."

Dr. Tim Hamon

Christian International Ministries Network

177 Apostles Way -OR- PO Box 9000

Santa Rosa Beach, FL 32459

850-231-2600

info@mailcimn.net

www.christianinternational.com

Additional Resources from Dr. Tim Hamon

Do you need breakthrough? Dr. Tim Hamon reveals key strategies from God in the Scriptures to show you how to move from the defensive to the offensive for effective breakthrough in this 3 CD Series teaching.

This timely message imparts "marching orders" to God's people now, revealing the significance of this time in history. Understand how the Church has been rebuilt and how God is now calling His people to rebuild our government, businesses, schools and churches according to His pattern. Single CD.

God is making a sound from heaven like a roaring lion. The Hebrew word for this sound is RUWA, which means a sound of blessing and breathrough. It is a sound of rejoicing and of war. Single CD.

Upon This Rock: The Kingdom and the Seven Mountains Leading in the Midst of Chaos is an audio teaching from Dr. Tim Hamon. 2 CD Series: *Roads of Reformation: Proven Models and Methods* is the first multi-author book on the topic of Seven Mountain Kingdom Influencers produced by CI Publishing. This is a book about change agents operating in one or more of the Seven Mountains of Culture that impact and influence society: business, government, family, religion, media, education, and entertainment.

Purchase products by Dr. Tim Hamon at the "Store" at www.christianinternational.com or call 800-388-5308.